The Old in Search of Avenues

notionpress.com

The Old in Search of Avenues

Haragopal P

Notion Press

Old No. 38, New No. 6
McNichols Road, Chetpet
Chennai - 600 031

First Published by Notion Press 2016
Copyright © Haragopal P 2016
All Rights Reserved.

ISBN 978-1-946204-68-4

This Book is Dedicated to the Memory of
My Dear Friend S.N. Sengupta

Contents

Preface

This book is a reflection of my experiences during the last sixteen years. It is not based on only extensive academic study and deep-rooted research. The knowledge gained by teaching students for the last ten years and the interaction with people in different countries during this period as a consultant post retirement contributed to these thoughts.

A few people, who are close to me, have helped me in editing and processing the information. I acknowledge them and convey my thanks.

The data was collected by interviewing people with a questionnaire and also informal conversations with persons across different economic strata and cultural backgrounds. This survey was also done in countries like Bangladesh, Japan, China, Russia, Sri Lanka and Ukraine. In these countries, it is not a statistically representative section of the population and the conclusions may not be fully objective.

In Vizag, a city in eastern India, retired people who walk on Ramakrishna beach every morning, elderly people attending lecture meetings of various god men and elderly people gatherings in the various parks in city constituted the target population.

We conducted classes for persons who were about to retire from government banks and public sector undertakings. The inputs from those participants were very useful.

In China, Justin, the driver of a car rental agency, was a very useful contact. He was conversant in English and put me in touch with displaced old farmers from Pudong. They spent their time playing cards and looking after grandchildren. Justin also introduced me to small traders in fish and vegetable markets in Pudong. He also explained how his mother spent her retired life looking after his son, watching Indian TV serials and playing cards. These were useful inputs.

In Japan, colleagues in Sumitomo Electric introduced me to several retired persons to help me understand their lifestyles.

In Bangladesh, we spent a few days in a place called Khustia on an assignment. We talked about and observed the obsession with religion among the retired people. They prayed *Namaz* five times a day without fail. Bengalis by nature are highly critical people and question everything. The older generation set aside this natural trait in matters relating to religion as it was a wonderful avenue to spend time.

A lot of input was obtained while conducting case studies to teach Business Strategy and Policy to students pursuing Management Education. *The Economist*, one of the most respected magazines, provided many useful articles on this subject. Social media inputs such as Facebook and the content in various blogs were useful to develop thoughts.

Stephen R Covey's books *The 7 Habits of Highly Effective People* and *The 8th Habit* were inspirational. His discussion on the Circle of Influence and Circle of Concern was so true in case of retired persons. In course of study, it was found that the majority of retired people were concerned about matters on which they should not be concerned about as those matters would not affect them. The various books written by Gurucharan Das, the eminent thinker and writer, had a great influence on me. One entire chapter deals with the problem of not being really truthful after retirement – You become what you are not.

This unwanted concern by retired people could cause many a problem for society as they have a great influence on the youth in developing attitudes.

Most of the people I have interviewed are from the city of Vizag. This city represents the modern India. It is cosmopolitan, young and people from all parts of India belonging to different economic strata live here and intend to settle here. People who came to this city for professional or business reasons find it a good place to permanently settle. The city also has a considerable number of foreigners from different parts of the world, and this influences the thinking of its citizens from a cultural perspective. We interacted with the parents of students at the time of admissions, and many of them were retired persons hailing from interior rural areas of Orissa, Chhattisgarh, MP, Jharkhand and Bihar.

The most interesting inputs were from those attending religious congregations in different parts of the city. The men and women who had taken part were mostly senior citizens. Interestingly, most of these persons had developed an interest in religion after retirement and their new-found enthusiasm was overwhelming. Many of these persons were suffering from diabetes, hypertension, kidney disease and other health problems associated with sedentary lifestyle and lack of physical exercise.

Why this book is called *In search of Avenues* has a nostalgic reason – my parents lived in Railway Bungalows. My father was a hardworking railway employee in British India. When the British left after Independence, a lot of opportunities were open to Indian employees. My father became an officer at an early age and was entitled to a bungalow. For most Indians from a lower middle-class background, this was a matter of great achievement and social prestige.

The allocation of bungalows occupied by the British with all the huge facilities was in a certain pecking order. The top officer's residence, clubs and recreational centers, exclusively for Englishmen, were in the First Avenue. They had huge gardens and the streets were broad and well kept. We had our residence in the Fourth Avenue at Kharagpur, a city in eastern India. During summer holidays, living with cousins in these houses was an interesting experience. We heard many stories about the lifestyles of earlier British occupants as told by servants. It was an object of curiosity and a scope for enquiry. These encounters developed an inquisitive mind and this book is the ultimate result.

The first five chapters relate to the facts collected through research and opinions of various authors related to this subject. The last chapter *Old Age as an Opportunity* is based on creative imagination. Dr Hemadri, FRCS, made many useful contributions to the writing of this book.

CHAPTER 1

In Search of an Avenue

In March 1996, I happened to be in Kolkata, a city in eastern India, on a business trip, and called my good friend Sachin Sen Gupta for a chat in the evening. We had many things in common – both of us started our career in the cable industry at the same company and shared the same values in life. Our families were close to each other as well. Sachin had two daughters who are of the same age as my daughters. He was working in Kolkata as the vice president of marketing in a leading cable company. His job called for frequent travel – both in India and abroad. He was a busy person and had very few hobbies – one of them being the violin, which he played every day for an hour whenever he was at home. His proficiency in playing violin is a result of ten years of serious study under the guidance of a prominent violin teacher in Jamshedpur.

We started the conversation over a glass of beer and it drifted to the topic of retirement and post-retirement, as he would be sixty years of age soon and I would attain that holy age after two years. He dismissed all apprehensions like economic security, health, his daughter's marriage and how to spend free time after forty years of hectic life. His passion was reading books on philosophy and his favorite authors were Bertrand Russell and

Nirad Choudhary. Bertrand Russell's *In Praise of Idleness* had a tremendous influence on him. He was convinced that idleness was bliss and should be thoroughly enjoyed. I could feel that all this bravado was to camouflage his deep feeling of insecurity due to his upcoming retirement. We parted, wishing each other the best.

On reaching Delhi, I got a call from him next day and the subject of discussion was again on post-retirement activities and his thoughts on many issues, the most important being how to spend time and the fear that he might not command respect from society once he retired. I consoled him by asking him not to worry and to derive courage by reading *In Praise of Idleness* again. After the call, the fears about post-retirement started disturbing me too.

One month before he retired, we happened to travel together from Singapore to Kolkata by Brunei Airlines Flight. Once again, the same topic came into focus – this time from an altogether different dimension. In those days, people who had only daughters were made to feel inferior. We were concerned about several imaginary situations such as 'Who will look after us when we become very old and need help? Who will look after our wives if we are crippled by a serious health issue? Who will light the pyre when we die?' and so on. There was some relief when the airhostess announced the in-flight entertainment: a French movie. There was a change of focus and we got out of our unpleasant thoughts by concentrating on the movie. It was about a famous French Chef who was decorated with several stars for his culinary skills. His dedication to the art of fine cooking led to many problems for his assistants in his restaurant. He was a perfectionist and hot-tempered and would throw away a dish if there was even a very slight deviation from the standards set by him. His assistants started attending meditation classes to overcome the constant tension in their job, but they still continued to work with him as they had a high regard for his culinary skills. In his single-minded devotion to make cooking a perfect work of art, he neglected the finances of the restaurant and got into problems with tax authorities, when they examined the books. He started getting impatient with his wife as she was looking after the accounts. All those crazy acts of aiming at attaining perfection resulted in the man having a heart attack and being admitted into a hospital. His daughter was the only person who stood firm in the belief that her dad's approach was always correct and she nurses him back to good health with all the love and total devotion to his ideals. This was an award-winning film and very well-directed.

We were greatly relieved and convinced that, in retirement, having daughters is a blessing and we should not bother about age-old social prejudices.

His phone calls were getting more frequent as the retirement date approached and most of the talk was about the search for various possibilities for spending the time available. On the day he retired, I wished him happiness and a long, peaceful retired life. He was silent and acknowledged my good wishes by mumbling some incoherent words.

On the second day after retirement, I received an early morning phone call. Sachin was in a state of great excitement his voice was completely different sounding as if a great ground-breaking discovery was made and I could not make out what he was saying. I listened with patience for quite some time and when he calmed down, I asked him to tell me slowly what had happened. I told him he was behaving like Archimedes when he had discovered the principle of floatation and went running naked through the streets of Syracuse, shouting *eureka*. He told me that his discovery was no lesser than that of the great scientist.

He described in detail about the developments during the first two days after retirement. On the day he had retired, when he reached home after all the farewell functions, his wife had a brief talk with him where she gently reminded him that he was now a retired person and should take some responsibilities at home, which she would elaborate on the next morning and advised him to take rest and restrict his whisky consumption.

He felt something unusual to hear such talk from a person who was docile and listened to him for many years without saying a word about his thoughts on philosophy, western classical music and the politics in his organization. He had a restless night and woke up early the next day, waiting to drink the tea that his wife had prepared for many years. There was no sign of it, and the first words he heard were a firm instruction from his wife that he must prepare two cups of tea, serve them on the table in the front veranda, and then call her. The job was done without a word from him, and while sipping, she told him to do a few things without fail. The first instruction was to collect milk packets, and the second one was to go to the nearby market and buy fresh fish and vegetables every day. The third instruction was to keep a watch on the cook. He was frozen in silence; it took thirty minutes to get back to normalcy. Never in his life had he woken up early to collect milk; also, going to market had never been in his scheme of things before getting married – such jobs were handled by his younger brother – and afterwards by his wife or his driver. By the time he recovered, his wife breezed in, and before leaving for the school where she worked as Head Mistress, she reminded him once again about the three assignments and left the house after bidding him goodbye.

The turn of events was disturbing and he thought of playing the violin to soothe his nerves.

Tolly, where my friend lived, was a recently developed building complex in a huge area of Kolkata. He had booked a flat while in service and was lucky to get that comfortable flat in the city. There was, however, a big deficiency in town planning in this part of the city, with reference to numbering of the houses. That part had been developed during the long years of misrule of the State of West Bengal, and Kolkata in particular, by the communist-led left-front government. The head of town planning was a political figure and unfamiliar with the complexities of urban planning. One of his foolish acts was to allocate house numbers to satisfy his friends and cronies who booked houses. In Hindu tradition, numerology has a great significance and certain number combinations are supposed to bring good luck. Being sentimental, some of the Bengalis wanted to have numbers associated with birthdays of eminent people like Rabindranath Tagore or Chittaranjan Das. The houses at Tolly were built over a long period of more than ten years. People who had financial clout built their homes earlier and some took a longer time to muster resources. All of these houses were built with government subsidies and there was a great demand. Most of the occupants were from the middle-class and higher middle-class. Whoever completed the houses got the numbers of their choice either by request or by pulling strings in the town planning department, headed by the ruling left-front party member. The result was a mess: a house whose number was 23 could have a neighbor with the number 4004.

Sachin had an early mover advantage. His flat was completed in the early stages and was a witness to the number mess that was taking place, but in the process, he was one of the few individuals who had a mental map of all the numbers of households in that huge township.

Once he had spent some time with the violin, he prepared another cup of tea and relaxed by sitting on his comfortable chair in the front veranda and observed a tired-looking person with sweat on his forehead and holding a paper in his hand, standing near the entrance gate and helplessly looking at him. He rushed towards the gate and gently asked him what his problem was. He narrated his agony: he was trying to locate a house without success for the past two hours, walking from one end of the township to the other and asking for help from several people. He was about to go back when a kind soul had recommended him to go to this house to seek help, along with advising him regarding the location by drawing a diagram and giving a few easily identifiable prominent landmarks. He also pointed out that if he failed to locate the house before 10 am, he stood to lose the opportunity of getting a job for his son. Sachin consoled him and assured him that the house would be located soon.

He accompanied him and navigated easily to the destination. He went back to his house and the gentleman came back to offer his thanks. Sachin asked him to sit down and offered him a cup of tea, then had a lengthy discussion about the bad governance and its effects on the society.

No sooner than he left, there was another man seeking his expertise to locate a house urgently, as somebody was seriously ill and the gentleman whose address he was holding was not answering the phone call. The same exercise was repeated and he spent a happy and satisfying four hours keeping busy. He did all the chores listed by his wife and planned to take a nap post lunch.

His second daughter arrived at his house before he could even start his lunch. She made enquiries about his health and other matters, sat down in front of him and gave a stern warning that he should lead the normal life of a retired man, and should not indulge in any idiocies associated with old people. She also warned him that if she came to know that he was causing problems, she would take him to Mumbai and he would have to look after her twin children, which would be a full-time job and he would be under her strict control. The language of the message was harsh but the inner core of it was full of concern and true love towards her father. She came close to her father's ear and told gently that she would telephone him every Friday evening at 7:00 pm and left immediately to catch her flight to Mumbai. She and her husband, a South Indian, were working in a bank at Mumbai.

These incidents of guiding a house's location to people in distress continued every day, and he was happy to find an avenue to spend time. He ultimately took an assignment to compose jingles for an ad agency after a few months. The point to be emphasized here is that it was not in the nature of Sachin to help people in distress. He valued his private space after busy working hours and could not care less if somebody had problem with locating a house. Retirement is a trigger for you to become what you are not, as explained in the next chapter.

Let us move to Vizag where I settled down after formal retirement. This is a place where we could enjoy tremendous local importance. There were plenty of relatives and members of the same caste living in this city and some were highly influential. The first thing I started doing after moving into my own house was to play golf regularly with three of my buddies. One day, after finishing the ninth hole, we sat in the clubhouse, sipping tea and the topic of discussion was rising prices. My partner Paddy asked me whether I knew the price of potatoes and onions at different markets. I explained my ignorance on this subject as the consumption by two of us living in the house was limited and made little impact on those expenses. I explained about the few occasions when even after I went to the vegetable market, the need for the price information had never arisen.

Paddy was disturbed and told me in a very authoritative voice that all the problems of tackling price rise were due to people like me who were not informed or concerned about the problem. He told me about how he had gone to four different places in town to get the price information and the fine differences in prices at the markets he had visited.

Paddy is a hardworking person with interest in sports. He worked for a long time in Dubai and brought up his children well, giving them excellent education in India and the U.S. He is retired and is comfortable with his finances and maintains a good standard of living. On further investigation, it was found that the price information was an avenue to spend the available time, and he cherished information and concern.

Moving to Bengaluru – where we spend two months in a year – some very interesting facts were observed. This city was a paradise for retired people once upon a time and still has a big percentage of retirees. Domlur is a suburb near an aircraft manufacturing unit. The factory has many housing colonies and small shops and departmental stores. The prominent road in the original part of this suburb has old independent houses on both sides. For buying vegetables and provisions, one has to go to this part of the suburb. During such visits, I used to observe an elderly person with a newspaper in his hand and a cup of coffee on the table in front of him, sitting on a chair in the front veranda of his lovely little house. He was always dressed in a casual south Indian dhoti and a vest and constantly scratched his feet and thigh. He used to sit there in the same position for a good four hours from 7:00 am to 11:00 am every day.

A deliberate attempt was made by me to get friendly with him and he wholeheartedly welcomed the invitation to interact. He described his past career as an accounts officer in the Auditor General's office. He had had a very successful career and a reputation for hard work, integrity, honesty and reliability. He got normal promotions, educated his children well and had a hectic schedule during his service. He always made it a point to dress well and was punctual. He had no active hobbies and was not particular about physical fitness and never made attempts to correct his sedentary nature of work with physical exercise. When asked why he was always reading a newspaper for four hours in the morning where the content space is quite small and most of the space is occupied by advertisements, he had a hearty laugh. He was frank to admit that, under the pretext of reading the newspaper, he was watching the people walking on the busy street in front of his residence. He admitted his helplessness in finding an avenue to spend the time available after retirement. He said that except for the light increase in blood sugar levels and early diabetic tendencies, his health was good. He indicated that he may take up active interest in tourism and visit places in India and in the US where his children are settled. He honestly admitted that he had never visited any place other than his ancestral village. He was never interested in history, culture or the geographical features of countries, continents, oceans, rivers, mountains, forests or any aspects of tourist interest.

In a corner departmental store at Domlur, a regular visitor at 9:00 am sharp was a veteran of the Indian Air force: retired Air Vice Marshal – a distinguished fighter pilot and a man of great accomplishment. He is an aged person, yet when he arrived at the shop he reflected the discipline that was imbibed in his system after a long tenure in the service. His purpose of the daily visit is to do the shopping of things written in a small piece of paper given by his wife. The next stop is the residence of his daughter, which was close by, where he would drink coffee and hand over things given by his wife. I was wondering how the requirement of two people called for a daily purchase of things. He was very clear when this question was asked and bluntly replied that this was a wonderful way of spending time. This decorated officer had never had a habit of shopping in his working life.

These real life observations were the motivation to go deep into the study of what post-retirement is, why a person becomes what he is not after retirement, what avenues he chooses to spend time in post-retirement, the power of the old, retired people as a potential gold mine to be used for social progress.

Technology, progress and the transformation of established systems are important factors in the lives of the older generation. Let us talk about the present generation of retired people. More than sixty percent of the retirees are not tech savvy. They are not familiar with emails, browsing and social networking over the net. They do not visit blogs or tweet. They do not use FaceTime, Skype or other facilities to communicate cheaply with their near and dear ones and miss a great opportunity to spend time. These advances are also closing other options for being occupied. In a recent TV interview, the CEO of a leading software company was describing how going to the post office to collect mail, and taking out an interest amount on senior citizens FDs were not required with introduction of automatic transmission of information through e-mail and smart phone. The important thing was, having a chat with the friendly post master, I became aware that it was a regular feature in the life of a retired person, which was being denied to elder people. Similar revolutionary changes are taking place in banking sectors. Electronic transfer of money and immediate updating of accounts when you withdraw money at ATMs and having information transfer through a cellular smart phone are making visits to a bank unnecessary.

In the earlier days, a very useful occupation for the older generation was spending time with grandchildren. I still recall my grandmother narrating the entire Mahabharata in daily installments and we eagerly looked forward to it. Today, children consider grandparents as boring and avoid them, resulting in closing of this option to spend available time.

The worst problem with many senior citizens is the perception that their presence was not being felt. This is true in many cases.

This imaginary assumption propels them to do all sorts of things to draw attention. The world is full of examples where proper handling of retired people has brought about many good initiatives to bring changes. This is dealt with in chapter three.

There is also a diametrically opposite dimension to the problems of the aged which we studied. In our sample were many brave soldiers and officers of the great infantry divisions of the Indian Army. One person stood out to offer a perfect example of old age without problems and simultaneously contributing to social progress. This soldier lived in a narrow lane close to the temple at the intersection of a National Highway and the Kailasgiri road that leads to National Highway. He had a commanding personality, tall and erect, but simple and well-dressed in the tradition of infantry soldiers and officers. He was in the temple everyday for an hour exactly from 4:00 pm. He stood in a dignified manner far away from the main deity and meditated for some time. It was a pleasure to watch this gallant soldier full of grace and calmness. I ventured to ask him what the reason for his daily visit to the temple was and the observance of silence and meditation. He hesitated for a while and told us in a slow tone: he prays for his departed comrades and officers who made their supreme sacrifice for the cause of their motherland. In the 1965 war, his regiment was in a border area and many of his colleagues had died in action. He spent the rest of his available time teaching the habit of cleanliness to youngsters living in his locality. He takes initiative to solve local disputes and educates the youngsters on the importance of physical fitness. In his own way, he asks his neighbors to be honest, straightforward and not compromise on their rights.

This interaction with that soldier of an infantry regiment was thought-provoking. Here is a simple retired soldier making an enormous contribution to society which is remarkable. He is not highly educated, and comes from a less privileged section of the society. He is a man without material wants and is highly satisfied that the Army is looking after its veterans. He was injured in action and yet never spoke a word about it. I recall the observation made by a professor of Harvard University Stephen Covey that character ethics are fundamental to human behavior and they are eternal. I talked about how the infantry soldiers and officers acquire these qualities, to my good friend and golf partner Retired Lt Colonel Sharma. He had a distinguished career as an infantry officer. He has seen action in Sri Lanka and in the Wars with Pakistan. He was injured in action and underwent many surgeries and went back into action. The Colonel explained that training and selection are the key elements. Exposure to battle conditions gives them unique qualities. To survive, they have to work together as a team where everyone is important. They develop a bond which cannot be described; respecting each other throughout their life is their tradition. They operate and live in an inhospitable terrain with elementary comforts and this translates into a character ethic of simple living and not craving for material wants.

Colonel Sharma is another example of an infantry officer with dignity, honor and simplicity. He lives in a place called

Sagar Nagar in Vizag. For a short time, he was running a security agency whose hall mark was excellent service. He is a person totally committed to the welfare of the under-privileged and his courage and outspoken attitude often landed him in occasional awkward situations. On one such occasion, he came to the rescue of a small vendor who had parked his cart in front of his house which was a restricted area. He found the traffic policeman harassing the vendor and making many unreasonable demands. He started arguing with the cop and told him that he was being unreasonable to the cart vendor. Police men in Vizag are efficient to attend a call made by their staff on duty immediately. An inspector arrived on the spot within minutes and got into the crowd, charged the Colonel for obstructing a policeman on duty and was on the verge of arresting him. His wife, who heard about the commotion, rushed to the spot and gently called the inspector aside and told him about her husband and the sacrifices he had made for the country, and finally, about his rank. The policeman immediately apologized to the veteran soldier and saluted him. Colonel Sharma has never talked about his rank and past achievements. He wanted to live with the people like an ordinary man and had never asked for any privileges.

In the suburbs of Vizag lies Boyapalem. I owned a plot of land and had to go there frequently to take care of it. During those visits, I had the privilege to observe happy fun-loving group of people, organizing cock fights. They are the veterans of infantry regiments and I included them in my sample for studying the activities of retired people. These people are different from that of the solitary soldier I described earlier. They hailed from the nearby villages, and as soldiers saw action in the wars with Pakistan, their occupation was to look after their lands and those of their officers who were allocated land by the state government for soldiers who saw action. They are totally devoted to their officers and made no distinction between theirs and their officer's lands. They gave the same respect and devotion and got the feeling as if all of them were still on active duty. Their equally important other duty was building character and imparting values of courage, discipline, physical activity, honesty, empathy and truthfulness to the village kids by example. Similar to Colonel Sharma and the solitary infantry soldier at Vizag, they never gave sermons to the village residents, never spoke of their past glories and everything was done by setting an example. They did have fun even at that age by organizing wild parties with lot of rum and lamb curry (in Coastal Andhra, no celebration is complete without fresh lamb curry). One of the redeeming features in this group is their lack of material wants. They are happy with what they have. They are proud of the Army and enjoy the rum they get from their canteens. They never forget their fallen comrades and hold remembrance meetings.

One of the finest experiences was the interaction I had with a retired veteran of an infantry regiment by name Colonel Rao. He was comfortably settled and was a satisfied person; his ambition was to teach young management students the importance of character and values which can transform society. He walked into my office and unfolded his plan. His child-like simplicity and honesty of the highest order was exceptional. In a plain way, he told us that he was not academically competent to teach management students. He explained that serving in infantry itself is an exercise in character building and that he would pass on that experience to youngsters. He then asked with humility what books he should read so as to get an academic base for teaching and that he would study them before starting the program.

I recall the words of my hero, the legendary soldier Field Marshal Sam Manekshaw. I was with him to collect the baggage in Mumbai's old airport. In those days, delays for baggage arrival were very common and I mustered courage to say hello and start a conversation. I was fresh from a visit to Bangkok where we had started a cable plant. Field Marshal Sam Manekshaw was very kind to listen to my views, and I explained how retired officers, who are qualified, were heading many industrial organizations in Thailand successfully. He was asked whether it could be done in India as the main driving force behind their success was discipline, total honesty, impartiality and hard work. The field marshal smiled and said that greater contribution could be made in character building by veterans settled across thousands of villages and towns spread all over India, if due encouragement was given.

These people with character never retire, in the true sense of the word. They are content, have no problems of *becoming what they are not.* They do not exercise power; their material wants are limited; they are honest, simple and straight forward; they exhibit courage throughout their life; and they enjoy true happiness by setting examples and inspiring future generations.

It must be remembered that many people across all sections of population have some impersonal interests in various fields of activity, and they pursued it after completing their regular jobs. These persons, after retirement from their jobs, focus on their personal interests for which they could not devote time during their service life. These are the fortunate who have a smooth transition; they also never retire till their health permits. They never become what they are not after retirement. The problem is they constitute a minority as per our study.

Our study at a management institute at Vizag gave useful insights. The director of this institute is a retired person. He was devoted to religion while in active service as a chemical engineer at various refineries all over India. His focus was very clear. He worked hard to put in his best efforts to do a good job and had never had big career ambitions. While in service, he visited all religious places and went to Mansarovar in Tibet, on three occasions, to get divine inspiration. He was regular in practicing *kriyas* (a ritual). Post retirement, he took up a job as an administrator at an eye hospital so that he could bring up his children. He continued part-time studies and got a master's degree followed by a PhD while doing a full-time job. He has no material ambitions and has room for both religion and academics in his schedule. He is at peace with himself and the immediate surroundings and is engaged in his passion for religion and teaching. His aim in last phase of his life is to transfer values of honesty, character, hard work and continuous learning to the younger generation.

The example of another institute established by Satya Sai (a religious leader) at Puttapurthi is ground-breaking. This is a part of a huge complex of educational institutes, a big hospital, libraries, and an ashram. In his lifetime, Satya Sai preached the religion of loving fellow human beings. A large number of people from India and all over the world visit the ashram to get inspiration as to how best one could serve their fellow citizens.

The management institute is headed by an eminent academician from a well-known All India Institute of National Importance. I went to meet him with a fond hope of getting a faculty position. He introduced me to faculty members and took me around the well-equipped library. This is one institute which is never advertised in media; they never approach any corporate bodies to take their students. The simplicity of faculty and students is the main feature of this great place and it is visible everywhere. A substantial number of researchers are eminent people who had retired from their positions. They are driven by passion, commitment and service to bring the students to a higher level of knowledge. There is a total absence of materialism. The faculty is given modest accommodation and spend their time in teaching, research and building character in their students. The students, after graduation, get into the world of business, practice integrity, honesty and other ethical values of the highest order. Here is an example of a large number of people making a smooth transmission to post retired life and contributing to society's progress like those soldiers of the infantry divisions of the Indian Army.

The examples result in few objective conclusions.

1) Retired senior citizens want to make their presence felt.

2) They have time at their disposal and are looking for opportunities to fill it to get satisfaction.

3) Some people do not retire; they either pursue the impersonal interests for which they could not devote much time while in active service and some have character ethics of the highest order and pass on the values till their death.

4) The paths chosen to occupy themselves for most of the retired persons are not in sync with their true nature. *They want to become what they are not.*

Chapter 2

Age

Age, as we all know, is measured by the calendar, that is, chronological age. Measurement of age by the calendar is appropriate for the purposes of documentation and records. It allows for comparisons between people. It allows reasonable and consistent thresholds to be set such as voting age, retirement age, juvenile/minor categorization for the legal system, driving age, recruitment ages, admission to educational institutions and so on. It is important to have such thresholds and benchmarks so that it provides equality and justice in the way society deals with people.

Hence, logically, people who are older by the calendar and might have retired are either tending towards being called elderly or are classed as elderly. Depending on the country and customs, elderly may have multiple meanings such as post-menopausal (in the case of women), being retired at the usual age for the country, having grandchildren, not being old by age but looking older per se or due to ill-health.

In the context of our discussion, on how chronologically older persons can contribute to themselves and to the society, it is relevant to look at the issue of age using concepts and lenses rather than calendar/chronological age.

How else can we measure or classify age? Are there other ways in which we can look at age?

Age from a Biological Perspective

Let us look at it from a reproductive perspective. The actual chronological age does have links with this as well, but from a biological point of view there is puberty, the reproductive phase and menopause (possibly andropause for men – but we will discuss this elsewhere). So, from a reproductive perspective, there are broadly three 'age' groups – pre-pubertal, reproductive and post-menopausal. The pre-pubertal is an absolute for both men and women; the reproductive age group is potentially absolute for men and women (potential due to the recognition of a variety of fertility issues and due to the decreasing chances as the phase moves on); the post-menopausal is absolute for women (unless greatly assisted by modern medicine), but the 'age group' or post-andropausal phenomena are not absolute for men (though it is of diminishing value in reproductive terms). Obviously, this categorization is simple because it is physiologically obvious and all of us can recognize it; the category is also very complex because of the personalization and variability. Interestingly, most things in life are also simple and complex at the same time.

Age from the Working Life Perspective

Age, in a professional or commercial context, in a way that relates to the workplace can be assessed by the duration of time spent in a particular activity (not necessarily in a particular title) or by experience gathered in the role. There is a difference between duration and experience. A person who has used the same equipment for many years is likely to have better knowledge on all or many of the aspects of that equipment than others who have not (such as new comers, senior appointments, foremen, managers, external consultants, etc.). A person who has seen various iterations of a process, service or product made, either using the same equipment or a series of different equipment, has experience (which is different from duration where repetitiveness is the operative phenomenon), which others will not have (such as fellow workers who have had repetitive work, fellow workers who have moved to other areas, fellow workers promoted to higher positions, new comers, managers, directors, etc.).

Age from a Wisdom Perspective

The Biblical history and mythology tells us that the earlier characters, around the time of Adam and Eve, lived to be 900 years or older. But, by the time of Moses and Joseph, the longevity was only about 100 years. In the Indian traditions, in the previous *yugas,* people were thought to have lived for hundreds of years, which has now become unbelievable in the present (Kali) *yuga.* Bhishma of Mahabharata times is believed to have lived up to 360 years.

Whether humans really ever lived that long is debatable. If we take the various scriptures literally, people may have actually lived that long. There are, of course, other explanations which are mathematical, like counting the lunar age (by month) and not by the Gregorian calendar we use these days. However, it is also eminently possible that the age could be and was measured in terms of wisdom. A community assigned your age according to wisdom. Even now or perhaps till recently, in the Hunza valley, people from the Burusho community assigned age by the wisdom of a person.

It is certainly possible that some of us have less wisdom, whereas some of us have more wisdom than the rest of our peers, irrespective of chronological age, education, status, wealth or work experience; sometimes, as a result of a combination of these. It is incumbent upon us and our communities to reflect on the issue of wisdom and assigning a value to it.

It is relevant to point out that there are many chronologically young persons, who are wise beyond their years, and many chronologically older people who do not seem to have wisdom – this issue is not about superiority of one person over another but about using every individual's wisdom to benefit themselves and their societies.

Longing to Retain Youthfulness

Most people, as they grow older in chronological age, try to present themselves in a youthful manner. Dyeing our hair is an example, or wearing a certain kind of makeup, for instance. In the western world and catching up extremely rapidly in the east, are things like Botox and plastic surgery. Why do some or many older people try to look younger than what they actually are? Next is the issue of trying to think and feel younger. It is not just about how one looks. Many older people want to be able to see, say, feel and do things typically associated with chronologically younger persons. The most recognizable example is that of male actors in their 40s, 50s and 60s, trying to portray roles that are half their age. For male actors, it is their livelihood and it is their profession to portray the role to the best of their abilities (including looks) so they do that. But many people do that in real life too. Interestingly, in working life, employers expect older employees to be as physically productive as a younger employee. They do this in the name of productivity, efficiency, output, etc. (by the way, employers should be looking at lifetime age-adjusted productivity, not doing so leads to unresolvable issues that are not the scope of this book).

A particular problem is that of physical manifestations of chronological age. A wrinkle or a wrinkled face is seen by many as at least unsightly or by some as "ugly." A chronologically old face is often seen as not beautiful. Interestingly, when we see our own parents aging and develop a wrinkled face, we see them as old but not ugly – for people close to us, there is a disassociation between old and unsightly, but at a societal level, there is an association between old and ugly. Even at a personal level (when we look at ourselves in the mirror), we often associate "old" with "unsightly" for ourselves (but not for our parents or perhaps for our children). This mental association causes harm to ourselves and to our society.

A person trying to look well-groomed is an issue of personal value – respecting your community and the importance of being hygienic – we are not talking about that. We are talking about the desire to look, feel and think younger. Why do we do that? Is that relevant or necessary?

We have to go back deep into history, spirituality and religion. If we look at any serious religious or spiritual figure in the past, it is almost exclusively young persons. If you look at eastern history and religions – every serious important entity was and is portrayed as a young individual – Lord Shri Ram, Lord Shri Krishna, every Vishnu avatar, Shiva, all the goddesses, Gautama Buddha. It is not easy to think of anyone in the older age group or look at any icon portrayed as an older figure. Jesus Christ died at thirty-six after a life that accomplished so much that is relevant till today. Prophet Mohammed's religious work was from age 40 to 60, while that is not exactly youth, in current terms it is still within a 'working age group' (but we must remember that his time was about 600 years after Christ). Adi Shankara died aged thirty-two. Unlike the times of World War II, western leaders are getting younger in chronological age (Bill clinton, Blair, Putin, etc) although eastern leaders tend to be from the older age group.

With this kind of history, background and legacy, it is simply entrenched into our minds for generations that youth is the age of "achievement." We begin to associate youth with success, beauty, achievement and all other positive attributes.

What we then do is we begin to fight our bodies and mind to somehow retain that youth for as long a time as possible. This is where we need to begin to differentiate. Using our body image to present a picture of youth or relative youth does nothing in terms of our ability to make any contribution to ourselves or the society; we only fool ourselves and others. Looking good to feel good (using the body to influence the mind) is marginally beneficial. However, if we used our mind to feel and behave in a way that increases our mind and body capacity, irrespective of chronological age that for some actually results in a body image that is youthful. Using the mind to influence the body is a better longer term tool that retains and enhances the ability to contribute to ourselves and to our society.

As your age changes, your contribution changes.

Human beings who are pre-pubertal do not contribute to the cause of reproduction. But their bodies and minds are constantly changing to prepare them to contribute for the next stage, which is the reproductive phase. That is how physiology works.

The problem with people as they get chronologically older is that most of the time the physiological changes are outward.

Is contributing to self and society a must?

Well, sometimes not contributing is the biggest contribution we can make; it can be of a greater good than contributing. It is relevant to contribute if we can create a positive effect. If our contribution is creating a negative effect, then it is best to withdraw or refrain from contributing. In any case, no one should be forced to contribute (the same way no one should be forced to have or not to have children when we are looking at the reproductive perspective of age).

Chapter 3

To Be What You Are Not

Living with grandparents from a young age offers a unique scope to observe behavior patterns of the retired old people. To study senior citizens in close quarters from the age of two to eighteen was by itself a great privilege. In my case, adding a further advantage was that my grandparents lived in the house of my grandfather's elder brother for five years. The house was huge and many old relatives were living with the two brothers, in keeping with old traditions.

My grandfather and his elder brother were people of the highest integrity. They worked very hard in their service career, were knowledgeable, simple and honest. The elder brother was one of the few Indian officers in the British-owned Indian Railway Company and by careful living, he acquired properties and settled down in a place named Berhampur. My grandfather worked in the same railway company at a lower level before settling in his brother's house. These two gentlemen had absolutely no post-retirement problems to spend their time. Their presence was felt in the family circles and the society around. Their house was also the center for intellectuals of the town to meet and discuss problems relating to freedom struggle and counseling people having domestic issues and property disputes. Life in pre-independent India was simple and people had few wants.

One of the pastimes for both these people was to spend an hour with me at an appointed time. I could get away by asking any questions in that period which may be very uncomfortable to them.

Their only odd behavior was their great admiration for the British. I had to hear very often that one should learn from the British – the discipline, punctuality, correct way of dressing and other qualities if India has to prosper. The elder grandfather would always be correctly dressed before settling down in his favorite chair at 6:00 pm. He will be surrounded by his *yes* men (veterans of world war) and his faithful servant will serve him his drinks as per strict instructions. On one such occasion, I bluntly asked him why he was so fond of the British way of doing things when our culture and traditions are equally good. He never replied and I could understand that I had crossed a line. After looking back now, I find the possible answer that it was his way of keeping himself occupied after retirement (Trying to become what you are not). His requirement to adopt this particular approach, which was extremely limited as he is a respected member of the society, and had significant social recognition and high character ethics. He was a role model for many persons, yet he had an inclination to behave like a British person at least for some time in a day.

A comparison to present day retirees is not much relevant as 24×7 news channels, laptops, smart phones and social media were not present in those days.

The training sessions organized for prospective retirees in government utilities gave interesting insights. Almost all the participants were confident (outwardly). They were self-assured and talked about their financial planning and how they had settled their children and have excellent relations with them. In the same breath, they were talking about inflation, raising prices and how difficult it is to factor them, children's aspirations and the changing social environment. The same confusion prevailed when we talked about their retirement plans. They had plans to be physically active, do regular yoga, concentrating on religious activities, taking interest in tourism, do a lot of reading and etc. When asked whether they indulged in these activities during their working life, most of them said no. All of them were confident that positive habits can be developed in a short period of time. Some of the post-retirement plans were exactly opposite to what they had done while in active service. People who had no great regard for religion wanted to be religious, people who had never read a book wanted to become voracious readers, people who had lead a sedentary lifestyle wanted to become fitness freaks, in short, they wanted to become what they were not after retirement.

We tried to tell the participants that habit is not an act but what you do repeatedly over a long period of time with passion. A habit represents true nature and personality of the individual. We examined each individual's strength and tried to give options, but it was not well-received immediately and probably provided food for thought. They were under the impression of transition from one stage to another in life, as propounded by Hindu philosophy, was a very easy path. Most of the participants wanted to do something after retirement which they had never liked doing in their service life and imagined that they would be able to change.

This is an exercise in fulfillment. Sadguru Jaggi Vasudeva says fulfillment is not attained by some action. At every stage of life, one thinks that if this happens, my life will become complete, and after some action, the ideas are thrown in the dustbin. The need to do something arises since your inner nature has not attained fulfillment. Your actions are not a result of your need, rather, it happens because you are in search of fulfillment. It happens with or without awareness. This is true in all stages of life but it is more significant in post-retirement stage. There is an element of guilt.

A person who has never prayed in the sixty years of his life and considers himself a highly rational individual, thinking praying is old-fashioned, cannot become religious after sixty years of age, and at best, it can only be a short term phenomena. In many cases, an element of guilt and fear of facing consequences comes to play. Indians are god-fearing people and practices like *mannat* (if a wish is fulfilled, a person goes to temples and shaves his head or make some offerings) is very strong even among highly educated people. People with health problems, domestic issues, bad monetary conditions and having a very big wish list, are tempted to bribe gods to get their problems sorted out.

Some of the specific areas of interest to retired senior citizens as per our study are:

Tourism

This makes a fascinating subject to observe. There are hundreds of senior citizens all over the world embarking on tourism.

Visiting places is an important step in learning. Mahavira, the founder of Jainism once said *Gyan* (Knowledge) is the sum total of learning plus *Darshan* (seeing places). Simply learning and studying or travelling to places will not give total knowledge. In this case were some senior citizens who wanted to become what they were not. Tourism is entirely for different reasons.

Tourism, in general, is something which gives fulfillment. A passionate tourist generally studies the place where he intends to go. He will become familiar with the history, geographical features, and cultural aspects of the place he intends to visit before making the travel plan. In the case of senior citizens, it is a matter of ticking one or more of the items mentioned in the hundred places you must visit before you die. The next satisfaction is to tell friends, relatives and acquaintances that they had been to a certain country or a place mentioned in tourist brochures.

In Shanghai, near the Bund area, cruise ships bring thousands of tourists, mostly elderly people from different countries. We asked about twenty retired American tourists about their interest in China. Most of them, excepting an elderly history professor, couldn't care less about Chinese history, culture, economy and similar things. When asked on whether they knew about important places like the Great Wall, Summer Palace, Tianamenen Square, Mao Tse Tung's Mausoleum, they just looked at the tourist guide book and waved their hand. These people would probably buy some curios and tell their friends and relatives that they had a great time visiting China.

It makes a great impression to say that I want to explore the world with a camera and see places. Many of the successful people, after making tons of money, retire early and travel to Africa to see animals migrating from Serengeti Plain, climb Mount Kilimanjaro, or enjoy a desert safari to Moroccan cities bordering Sahara. Some of them go to the Amazon River basin in Brazil and such other exotic spots. The tourism industry is the most organized entity with a strong advertising focus. It makes a great impression on the senior citizens, who have plenty of time at their disposal. People like to imitate hugely successful people, and it is another driving force behind the enormous interest in tourism. There are many countries like Switzerland, France, Italy, Egypt and Kenya, whose economies are dependent on tourism; the state promotes the cause by investing in infrastructure and facilities. The success of Kerala being promoted as *God's Own*

Country and the recent promotion of Gujarat as a tourist destination is a man-made effort with the help of technology and media to promote tourism.

It is an accepted fact that all tourists do not do research on the places they visit, and enjoy knowing just the basic facts about the place. The relaxation element is very important and the joy of discovery is not measurable.

I recall another significant family tour of Europe conducted by Thomas Cook, with many hailing from Gujarat, Delhi and the South. It was a tight program as all the participants (mostly senior citizens) were interested in visiting the maximum number of countries in Europe and not particularly concerned about enjoying the aspects of culture, cuisine and natural beauty at leisure. The tour brought us to the historic city of Paris, steeped in rich culture and the birthplace of the modern world. Most of the people in the group were not impressed by Paris, by the time we reached our destination, the Louvre Museum, the most important landmark of Paris. The guide asked us to enjoy the museum visit and to his astonishment, nobody other than the two of us, expressed a desire to see the Louvre. Adding insult to the injury was the active shopping of all the participants, in the small shops located opposite to the great museum owned by *Sindhis* from India selling odds and ends.

Religion

This is one thing that most of the Indians think is the right activity to be pursued with full intensity only after you retire. In the Hindu way of life, an organized religious hierarchy to preach and perform religious activity is totally absent. This provides enormous scope for plenty of people with the gift of the gab to give discourses on the Bhagavad Gita, Vedas, Upanishads and other religious texts. In eastern philosophy, you can interpret matters related to theology in a number of ways; this gives the opportunity to anyone with sketchy knowledge to speak and give discourses. These demagogues have a captive audience in retired people who think that they are becoming religious by being regular listeners to their fiery speeches on dharma and related subjects. This is a way to spend two hours every day, in an attempt to become religious.

We tried to do some research on this important aspect of every Indian's life. Our study was limited to Hindu society. In the city of Vizag, there are many big halls where the religious preachers address their devoted audience. Our repeated visits to one such gathering confirmed that an overwhelming audience consisted of senior citizens, both men and women. Properly dressed volunteers guide the devotees to the areas meant for men, women and VIPs. There is a strict segregation of sexes and they are not supposed to engage in conversation with each other. The initial rituals and prayers are conducted with utmost solemnity and the stage is set for the arrival of the reverend speaker. Pizza Baba (In our family circles, he is known by this name for his weakness for pizzas) arrived in an austere manner, the environment perfect for effective communication and had all the prerequisites to get audience attention in the take off stage of the discourse are in place. Pizza Baba stared at the audience, smiled and offered namaskar. The subject of discourse chapter three of the Gita is forgotten by the audience, and everybody's mind is occupied with the dashing presence of the young speaker who is handsome and charming, with an excellent physique. There were murmurs of appreciation for the speaker. All the initial efforts resulted in a perfect opening for his discourse and he cruised along with eloquence for two hours by adding the right doses of humor, relating true life examples and posing questions to the audience. There was never a dull moment, and he made a smooth landing at the end of the discourse with an impressive modulation of his voice.

Pizza baba excelled in communication skills. More than the content, it was the impressive delivery which had a magical effect on the audience. We asked the participants a few questions about what they understood in those two hours. Most of them brushed aside the question and advised us to appreciate the impressive delivery, and said that religion was a matter of faith and not a knowledge-gathering exercise. They also emphasized that, in Hindu faith, listening to the Gita is by itself a religious act.

A good number of them had liberal values towards societal norms and were not religious, but surprisingly, every one of them felt that one must pay a lot of attention to spirituality and understand dharma, karma, soul, body and mind.

We asked them about Swami Vivekananda's view on Hinduism, on the importance of yoga to maintain a healthy body, which was the first step to be religious, on the importance of control of *Indriyas* (five senses), on being free from wants, on developing attitudes of giving and being non-attached.

The replies were vague, and we could infer that most of them enjoyed good food and do not do yoga or any other form of exercise. In the South, not long ago, a fat body with a belly was associated with success and prosperity.

A lot of data was collected from a representative sample from around six thousand people, who walk on the road adjoining the beach every day at Vizag. This is one of the success stories of the municipality of this beautiful city. This road is a stretch of four kilometers and is vehicle-free for three hours from five o' clock in the morning and relatively pollution-free as it is a 'no plastic' zone. It is an initiative of the citizens and gives hope that it is possible to do orderly things in India and everything is not chaotic. A large number of senior citizens walk regularly on this road. Some of the senior citizens walk with their wives and some walk alone. We focused our attention on these two groups, confined to couples where the husband and wife were both alive and covered the entire economic strata. The most interesting facts that came to light were that the husband and wife team who walk together are relatively healthier and are not obese, and they are also free from diabetes. The senior citizens (men and women) who walk alone comparatively have more health problems and have acquired them recently. They also developed, after retirement, a religious bent of mind and are regular in their attendance at religious discourses. They are recent adherents to social causes that propagate so-called moral values, and spread the message of limited interaction of men and women in public places, convinced that all the problems women face are due to free mixing and the influence of western values spread by media.

Going deep, one wonders why there is this change in perception. Indications are that they are due to psychological reasons. This is a matter which has to be researched and it could lead to interesting conclusions.

Sadguru Jaggi Vasudeva, in stressing the benefits of yoga, stresses the importance of union, starting from the folding of hands to the togetherness of things which brings peace, harmony and happiness.

In the field of management, the trend is a teamwork of combined efforts, which is replacing the old concept of glorifying and rewarding individual achievement.

Companies such as Boeing practice the team approach very effectively, and many are adapting as there is a positive benefit and motivate people for achieving excellence. The saying *1+1 becomes 3 in team work* has been found to be effective. Togetherness is strength, happiness and respecting each other.

After extending this concept to families of retirees where the husband and wife both are alive, and on connecting it to our observations on morning walkers, some conclusions are obvious:

For the senior citizens who walk alone, something is missing. Families are the basic building blocks of the society, and togetherness in physical mental and spiritual sense is a highly desirable ingredient for happiness. It is possible that a sedentary lifestyle and lack of control in eating habits will lead to a point in one stage of life, where one becomes incapable of being close to his life partner, and this manifests in developing perceptions of morality and changes in earlier attitudes when they were physically normal. The only explanation for becoming overnight champions of morality and character assassination of people who are normal, is a result of this development. The non-controversial truth is true love is permanent and is irrespective of the health of either of the partners, but a self-inflicted health problem due to factors such as alcoholism, smoking, bad eating habits, lack of exercise is a different dimension. Research is needed in this area of human interaction.

Next to tourism and religion, the favorite activity of many a retiree is to indulge in social service. Many of the retirees are doing an excellent job by actively participating in good causes such as volunteering their services for charitable dispensaries, child clinics, old age homes, legal aid to the old and similar causes. A good number of people participating in such causes are silent non-actors and they are satisfied with being in the group without doing anything. They want to be known as active participants in a good cause, and many believe that the world is full of wrong things and they have a duty to set them right. They are a concerned lot and embedded deeply in the circle of concern, not knowing they have little influence to accomplish this.

In the last decade of the twentieth century, the movement of women's liberation was sweeping the west, and its effects had an influence on educated Indian women. In India, the position of women was totally different from what it is today. Women keeping with eastern values considered bringing up children and running of the house as their main job. The media was not strong and active in bringing women's issues to the center stage. The women's liberation movement was however felt by half-educated upper-class women in the city of Jamshedpur, an industrial city in India. They were mainly older women and had a lot of time at their disposal. Their husbands were mostly retired/working executives in the factories. These well-to-do people felt that there are many grievances among women, to which society is not paying any attention and plunged into action by forming an organization to project their grievances in a local club. In this meeting, a local journalist suggested to the group that if they have a person among them – a woman with academic distinction, then the movement would get a greater mileage. The head of the department of research and sociology of one of the leading management institutes located in the town was their obvious choice. This professor had many academic distinctions to her credit. She had a PhD from a leading university in America and she is recognized worldwide as an authority on social welfare. The women's group got an appointment with her for discussion.

The professor, being an academician, made a study of the profiles of the participants. She concluded from the various research papers submitted by the students that the biggest exploiters of women, are the women from the upper strata of society in this town. To start with, they had full-time servants, who were not given weekly off days. The servants were asked to work continuously for long hours, which are prohibited by laws of the land. They were exploited in many other ways and not treated properly. These servants were women belonging to various local tribes, and they were poor and had no voice to represent in any of the government bodies looking after the welfare of the citizens. A few of the older members of the women's organization had many imaginary grievances against men and assumed that they were the common problem for all women. A few women of this upper-class also assumed that women's liberation movement was all about having freedom of sex and sanction to have affairs and multiple partners.

On the appointed day, these fashionable well-dressed ladies walked into the study of the professor who was well-prepared for the event. She appreciated their noble cause and requested their president and secretary to make a presentation. The president of the organization – a lady in her seventies – was a commanding figure. She led a luxurious life and was an active member of all clubs in the town whose exclusive membership was restricted to senior executives of various factories. She was one of those persons who were convinced that she served her husband, brought up her children and sacrificed many things. On the retirement of her husband, a docile gentleman, she thought the appropriate thing to do was to get into the driver's seat on family matters and do things such as sending her retired husband to the vegetable and fish market everyday by bicycle to get fresh produce and giving the responsibility of dropping her at various places every day and pick her up at the correct time. In her presentation, she highlighted the so-called problems of the exploited women in Indian society, and how, under her leadership, she will implement remedial measures. The other speakers stressed similar views and requested the professor to join them in this good cause.

The professor listened to them and asked each member to answer few questions and assured them that she would join on the condition that the minimum requirements are met adequately. Her first condition was that, for any proactive initiative, to bring about improvements, the group of members must come from families where there is love, respect and togetherness. There was a pin-drop silence and intense soul-searching as none of the members fulfilled this pre-requisite. She gently told them to take their own time and come back later, if necessary. She knew perfectly well that these women wanted to become what they were not. They had no interest in fellow women problems, and suddenly after becoming senior citizens, they wanted to become crusaders to solve the problems of the poor women whom many of their members were exploiting. The new-found enthusiasm was not genuine and sincere; it was essentially an exercise in keeping themselves engaged and getting attention. There are many organizations which render very useful service to the society, and their members are committed to a cause, right from their formative years, and the tendency to serve society is not an overnight development.

Dependents of People of Indian Origin

One of the most fascinating sections of senior citizens is the dependents/relatives of people of Indian origin in the U.S. A large number of such people are spread in western and southern India. We studied the large group of such people staying in the city of Vizag, and this group, to a fair extent, represented the entire segment living in different parts of the country. To start with, they assume that they are part of a superior sect of the population, and they know everything about America. Some of them do have a great knowledge about American history, and they know of Columbus's adventure to discover India that had led him to discovery of West Indies. They also know about his ship, the Santa Maria, and some historic events like the Civil War, the Oration at

Gettysburg, the Boston Tea Party, the Fourth Amendment and Teddy Roosevelt. To know about American history or anything about America is not expected from middle-class Indians, whose children had prospered by migrating to the United States of America. Most of these dependents command a crowd of people whenever they return from America and give a discourse on the great wisdom of Americans on every front. They talk about traffic discipline, roads, skyscrapers, cars, how they drink whisky with crushed ice and so many other things. Many Indians, even today, are not knowledgeable about the U.S., and they pray and hope that one of their children would go to the U.S. and bring prosperity to their families.

The unreasonable part of it is to boast about their American visits, which primarily are to look after the grandchildren especially at the time of delivery of babies, and after delivery, enable their daughters or daughter-in-laws to work, leaving their young children in their care. America attracted immigrants as per their necessity as a deliberate act of state policy.

To start with, they brought slaves from West Africa when cotton production was booming, there was little mechanization in agriculture and it was mostly manual labor. In the initial period of industrialization, they welcomed Germans, Italians and other Western European citizens. They welcomed Filipina nurses when the healthcare industry started booming. For some time, they encouraged Russians intellectuals to emigrate for political motives (to cause a disruption in Russian society and accelerate the collapse of communism and division of Russia).

The enormous effort to boost the presence of Chinese and Indian students in American universities was a step to strengthen the finances of those educational institutions. Most of the universities took in students who could not gain entry into the top educational institutions in China and India.

The latest craze is mass migration of engineers in all disciplines to do a software-related job in the U.S. America needed men with a rudimentary engineering knowledge to occupy thousands of vacancies in software customization and development. These jobs were boring, repetitive and against the basic nature of Americans who were eternally in search of discovering things and looking for adventure. The Indians or most of the marginally qualified Indians fit into the situation. The scenario is similar to the days when there was farmworkers' shortage to cultivate cotton or the shortage of workers capable of working near the furnaces of steel melting shops in Detroit or the hospitals without sufficient nurses situation.

A university professor described it nicely by saying that an overwhelming majority of Indians working in the U.S.A are a commodity. To the parents of these youngsters, they were the heroes, earning sixty thousand to seventy thousand dollars a year which was beyond their wildest imaginations. These parent groups have one cause to pursue – advising people who aspire to send their sons and daughters to the U.S.A. – The land of happiness, prosperity and everything a human being wants is in America. This is followed by talk on poverty in India, the land of filth, and how people are not following traffic rules and how they do not slow down before schools and emphasize repeatedly that there is no future in this country. These groups have become so large that they have formed associations and have regular get-togethers. They are spending old age fantasizing things. While living in this city, no one can escape them. You will have to listen to their stories about getting ten-year visas from the U.S embassy, how someone illegally got into the U.S and some imaginary talk about things in U.S.A.

A questionnaire was given to many persons who had been to the U.S.A., talking about various aspects of American life authoritatively. The results were amazing – not one person could answer all the questions correctly, and only a very few were able reach fifty percent score. The conclusion was obvious – these older citizens have found an avenue to spend the time that was available with them in abundance. They were getting recognition, and they wanted to be what they were not – Authority on America.

Let us examine why the age-old strongly-held Indian value that transformation should take place once a person attains old age is not happening. The word *transform* is well-explained by the eminent author Dr Wayne W Dyer. It is essentially going beyond the physical dimension of your form. The physical part of you is only one percent which is essentially your body – flesh, bones, height and weight. It is the outer package of the total being. Ninety-nine percent of you is your intellect and conscience, your will to do and other intellectual abilities. During the early part of life, due to today's materialistic society, there could be a compelling reason to concentrate more on the less important aspect, to be practical and get along with the vast majority of the people by attending the physical aspects. Once you are retired, as per our ancient Indian traditions, you are supposed to make a deep examination of your inner self and make efforts to use your ninety-nine percent of the invisible form of yourself. This will bring eternal happiness and prevent you from indulging in actions which disrupt the society and disturb harmony.

The retired infantry soldiers I described earlier are exactly doing the same. All their actions are for social progress, utilizing the power of the aged in a constructive way. They never made a deep study of the psychological dimension of transformation after retiring, and their actions are by default. It is due to the training and experience during their active service, where harmony and togetherness were essential for survival, and they continued that journey in their later years. A large number of retirees do not fall in this category; their concentration was on physical form throughout their working life. Why it is so is the natural question.

As per Dr Dyer, the resistance to transformation is essentially fear; he calls it 'head-in-the-sand' approach to your own spirituality. The older citizens that we studied till now are torn between forms of their thinking. On one side, they want to be spiritual, that being the reason for their futile pursuit to be religious by attending discourses of various spiritual gurus. On the other side, their strong attachment to materialistic things and lack of attention to disciplined habits like moderation in eating, and lack of physical exercise over their entire working life will undo their efforts to be spiritual.

Dr Dyer states that a transformed being is incapable of behaving in a non-spiritual way towards others. This could be the main reason for indulging in endless activities that are not in keeping with their true nature. Spirituality begins with the assessment of oneself in an extremely honest way and not bothering about what others think and script your plan of action to keep engaged once you attain old age. One has to translate thoughts into reality by being the writer, director and producer by constant self-examination.

A personal transformation by focusing on the hidden powers of human beings by being spiritual is the best approach for happiness in old age. Studies show that one develops qualities such as tendency to think, ability to smile easily and act spontaneously with experience and also lose a few characteristics such as loss of interest in judging others, loss of interest in interpreting the action of others, loss of interest in conflicts, loss of ability to worry. These are exactly the abilities which retired people with plenty of time at their disposal do not indulge in and are the cause of many problems in society.

CHAPTER 4

Power of the Old

THE GENERAL IMPRESSION ALL OVER THE WORLD IS THAT older people give a lot of advice which is mostly irrelevant. The rapid growth in technology had changed many things, and one such thing was making the shelf life of thoughts, ideas and developing ways of doing things very short. The pace of change is getting faster, and in such a situation, senior citizens whose ideas were relevant in their days are no more significant. The reality may be right, but human weakness refuses to accept it. In eastern countries, having values include the strong respect for wisdom associated with age. We listen to the old with obedience; we never question them.

The power of the old is best explained by going through the lessons of history in the recent past in China and Russia. A historic land mark, in human development in the late twentieth century is the making of modern China. It was an earth-shaking event. China, in two decades, became the manufacturing capital of the world. The country became the second super power in the early twenty-first century. In GDP terms, it will overtake United States in the near future. It is also marching towards democracy respecting civil liberties in slow steps. There is no poverty absolutely, and the society will get a total healthcare system on par with western countries.

All these things are happening from the year 1957 mainly due to the determined efforts of one individual Deng Xiaoping, the architect of modern China. In the most researched book on modern China by Ezra Vogel, we find that Deng's overriding priority was to take the older generation into confidence in each step leading to the liberalization process. The biggest challenges he faced from 1978 till his death in 1997 were mostly from the powerful old hierarchy in the political arena. There are a large number of essays and thesis on implementation from management institutes all over the world. In almost all the countries, whether they are democracies or functioning under authoritarian rule where there is limited democracy, the problem is implementation of plans formulated after a lot of thought and discussions.

In a country like the U.S. or India, they are derailed in one of the House or due to internal sabotage by parties, whose financial interests will be affected by implementing the planned agenda. Americans always respected strong presidents, and they could easily overcome obstacles and implement policies. Generally, a strong president in the American context is one who makes quick decisions, takes action that are visible to the American public and in keeping with the Wild West traditions of America, is extremely bold whether it is required or not, irrespective of consequences. American presidents are traditionally surrounded by *yes* men who helped them to get elected. After elections, a good number of these guys are accommodated as ambassadors, White House staff, and in jobs where they do not do anything and contribute to budget deficits in American economy. All the presidents before Obama, with the exception of Ronald Reagan, followed this sacred tradition and had old trusted *yes* men who advised the presidents to do some so-called brave manly acts to keep the public under spell and do things which they wanted to do. In Obama's case, the tradition was kept with the only difference that these cronies were younger in age.

In this process, the advisers advised to intervene in Korea, Vietnam, Cambodia, Somalia, Iraq, Haiti, Serbia, Libya and many such countries. The Americans bombed these defenseless countries and caused immense harm to the civilians and many Americans died in the process. Clinton was a clever man in this bunch; he targeted Serbia and Haiti (indiscriminate bombing of Serbia where even the Chinese embassy was partly damaged and in Haiti the marines landed as if the situation is similar to allied troops landing in Normandy).

Dutifully, the American media covered the events with great detail, glorified the achievements of the Marines and the heroism of the bomber pilots. Clinton achieved his purpose with the least cost and effort to command the American people's respect as a strong leader and continued his activities without difficulties. The other presidents like Bush (senior and junior), Lyndon Johnson, and Nixon followed the wise old men's advice, and went to war with Iraq, Vietnam, Afghanistan and also bombarded Somalia and Libya for no earthly reasons. They achieved the sacred objective of impressing upon the people that they were strong leaders, but caused havoc and brought radical fundamental religious extremism to the forefront, which could have been brought under control by the dictators ruling Iraq and Libya and Afghanistan.

Carter was a typical case of showing the so-called American definition of strong leadership by bombing some defenseless country but he made half-hearted attempts to drive Russians who had influence over the Afghan dictator with the help of extreme radical religious fanatics from all Muslim countries.

The ruler of Afghanistan was secular, controlled terrorists and never posed threat to anyone. The damage caused by this action will continue to hurt the world till the middle of the twenty-first century.

Reagan was the only president who never had to do anything spectacular to show his strong leadership. He gave less importance to his old advisers and depended more on his abilities to communicate sternly and effectively. Gorbachev feared his strong message to break the Berlin wall to such an extent he not only broke the wall but also ended the Cold War. To sum it up, the American way of successful political achievement was through spectacular acts prompted by old advisers. Obama brought an end to violent acts to prove strong leadership and depended on demagogy and creating an old boys club of elites of top universities who mastered the skill of presentation, and the American public, being less intellectually inclined listened to him in awe and for a time were convinced that a messiah has landed in America to solve all their problems. They realized it was a sophisticated act too late. However, he had the distinction of not bombarding any country severely during his regime to establish credentials of strong leadership.

In China, the problems Deng faced to introduce reforms were more severe than what an American President faces to establish himself as strong leader. For a while, Deng also was inspired by American Presidents after his close association with Henry Kissinger and Nixon. He had another inspiration at close quarters. Mao made a quick strike at Indian forces on the Tibetan border to nip in the bud any support to Tibetan dissidents from India. He called it a mission to teach India a lesson and the withdrawal of Chinese forces was also equally swift. Mao made sure that it was not given any media or public attention. Even today, if you ask any old Chinese academicians about this intrusion, they will tell honestly they were not aware of it. Mao had no necessity to impress the Chinese public. He was popular and had full control, his objectives were just different: to reduce Indian influence which was strong among Tibetans. He kept it away from public attention as he knew the average Chinese citizen in spite of dictatorial and authoritarian rule was sympathetic to India and it would have created a backlash.

Deng inspired by his association with American influence thought of applying the same business model to establish him as a strong leader before carrying his reforms. He had a great opportunity. Vietnam was getting closer to Russia; its influence in Cambodia was enormous. Deng thought that this was an opportunity to establish his authority as a strong leader. He intended to teach Vietnam a lesson similar to what Mao did to India. He forgot in this process that the comparison was wrong. Mao's intention was to send a strong message by surprise intrusion for a temporary period. He kept it secret from his own people before and after the intrusion. He was fully aware of negative repercussions of this act from international perspective and from his own people. He was fully aware of the limited American response, as at that point of time America was actively supporting Chinese anti-Russian policies. Deng mustered disproportionate forces to attack Vietnam, and finally, when the attack took place, it resulted in a humiliating defeat for Chinese forces in the hands of battle-hardened Vietnamese.

The entire exercise was based on wrong presumptions. The American model of establishing authority based on some so-called spectacular act was in synch with their culture, while colonizing the country and the onward march to the Wild West, the leadership was in the hands of reckless adventurers and fortune seekers. There were no checks and balances and most of the original population was wiped out by occupation and violence without any regret. The United States had no long history or homogeneous society, and being separated from the rest of the world, such action is possible to establish leadership.

For Deng, to replicate this in China, to kick-start the reform process was irrational. Vietnamese leaders like Ho Chi Minh and Gen Giap were highly respected figures in China. China also backed the Vietnamese National Liberation struggle against France and the U.S.A. Deng was a fast learner and very quietly under-played this misadventure and laid plans to introduce reforms that would propel him to great heights in leadership. He was a great observer of human behavior and worked closely with many decision-makers during Mao's chairmanship. He also enjoyed Mao's trust in implementing "The great leap forward" to propel China as a country that would be in the forefront of manufacturing. No doubt it was a failure but this symbolic act put a permanent impression in the minds of the Chinese people that they would be the center for manufacturing for the entire world. He was an active player in the *Let Hundred Flowers Bloom and Hundred Thoughts Prevail* program and carefully recorded the opinions of key personnel in the Communist Party hierarchy. He, along with Mao, initiated the *Learn from the Masses* program.

It was unfortunate that he became a victim of this when Mao doubted his loyalty and sent him for a while to be with the masses as a tractor plant mechanic before he was rehabilitated back into power. He also supported with less enthusiasm, *The Great Cultural Revolution*. Deng, being a wise man and keen observer in all these programs initiated by Mao, noted that the key players were the aged Liberation Army veterans with their immense hold on party machinery and followers. Mao depended on them for every initiative excepting the Cultural Revolution. In implementing the Cultural Revolution, Mao was depending on his wife and Red Guards, the rowdy crowd of youngsters inspired by his thoughts. This movement was a total failure causing immense harm to the society, and ultimately lead to the death of Mao Tse Tung.

Deng learnt a great lesson that in the prevailing circumstances, nothing could be done in China without the active support and blessings of old veterans of the party, and importantly they could silently destroy any initiative even when it had the sanction of mighty statesmen like Mao.

It must be remembered in spite of the deliberately wrong propaganda of western media, a large number of people I talked to during my many visits to China ardently believe the theme of the Cultural Revolution – *smash four olds — customs, culture, habits, ideas* – was very relevant, and it was primarily responsible for turning China into a modern nation. Had the implementation been done with the old veterans' full cooperation and involvement, it would have been a great success.

Reforms in theory were very simple, essentially unleashing the tremendous entrepreneurial talent of Chinese people with the help of western capital. The challenge was implementation and Deng's answer was to use the power and influence of the old. Deng also had full confidence that reforms would change the face of China. He however had some fear that it may fail, and as a precaution, initiated the reform process in a remote underdeveloped area close to Hong Kong – a British colony at that time – in the Guangdong Province. It was a success beyond anybody's dreams and an earth-shaking event which ultimately made China the world's manufacturing capital.

I had the opportunity to talk with my good friend Zhi Ping Xue, a communist and close to the Shanghai Party leadership, in those days when Deng was the paramount leader. He told me a few months before his death that Deng had told his inner circle of friends about his deepest regret. When asked what that was, Deng explained that his fear of failure lead to the start of the reform process in the distant Guangdong Province. Had it been started at Shanghai, China would have achieved the same success at least ten years earlier.

This shows the power of the old and what they are capable of achieving or destroying. Deng's other important contribution to stability was the way he handled the Tiananmen Square development. China was about to plunge into chaos and disorder, but he never acted on his own. He took the counsel and support of marshals of the PLA (People's Liberation Army) in the standing committee, retired marshals and generals before ordering crackdown. On one side, it was a democracy movement popular among the Beijing citizens; it was led by university students and intellectuals. On the other side, discipline was breaking, the party's hold was weakening, and the support of one senior Army veteran would have made it extremely powerful and may even end the Communist Party's hold over Chinese masses. Deng's wise old method of involving old veterans of the party saved the situation.

Compare the situation with that of the Soviet Union while in transition from the communist rule to a failed liberal state. Gorbachev never took the old veterans of the Communist Party into confidence and was more dependent on pro-American advisers. This resulted in a chaotic situation, and in this process, the Soviet Union was fragmented and became a third world country from a super power, and in any case, the democracy and western modern values were never achieved.

The power of the old has been demonstrated in many societies with many positive outcomes. The problem with technology moving at a fast pace is causing disruption of existing way of doing things and in many cases, bringing new dimensions in thinking. This is a threat to the power of the old. One way of countering this development is continuous updating, and many senior citizens are doing it effectively. The overwhelming majority of the retired people does not change but is still powerful, and if they are not kept engaged, they will exercise that power in wrong direction. The scenario in the twenty-first century with respect to demographic developments calls for a serious thought. Almost forty to fifty percent of the population in the developed countries and in some developing countries will be aged over sixty. No country can have a sustainable social security model, where fifty percent of the working population is made to support fifty percent of the idle population. The other development is the rapid advancement in medical sciences which is increasing life expectancy. People are becoming health-conscious, and some are healthy and capable of working for many years beyond sixty. The last chapter deals extensively with this subject. On the technology front, the birth of the fourth industrial revolution has already begun. It is a destructive model which will bring in fast computing, energy storage devices, robotics, 3D printing, solar and fusion energy developments, electric cars and rapid advancement in genetics and new approaches to medicine. The repercussions on the old would be enormous. New models of keeping the senior citizens occupied from the technological and social perspectives would also emerge.

We have to take advantage of the power of the old. They are responsible for the successful transformation of China from poverty and backwardness to a modern nation. They are responsible for establishing democracy and stability in India. The rebuilding of war-torn Japan and South Korea was mainly the result of the senior citizens' wisdom and the respect given to the elders in those societies. The success of Vietnamese liberation and unification of the country after a glorious fight was led by

Ho Chi Minh and Gen. Giap, the grand old leaders. The effect of not using the power of the old has also caused immense harm to the society at many places. The entire Arab world is in turmoil mainly for not giving due recognition to the old.

Let us start with Iran, a modern, educated society that prevailed in this country at the time of Mohammed Mossadeq, who was overthrown by Shah with active help from western countries. In Iran, the clergy played an important role, in their enthusiasm to establish a western model society by Shah and his supporters, they ignored Ayatollah and this resulted in a suppressed anger and resentment, which eventually lead to replacement of Shah by a theocratic society headed by Ayatollah Khomeini. Iran, which was heading for a modern state, was thrown back into a fundamentalist state. The young dictators starting from Nasser in Egypt, Saddam in Iraq, Assad in Syria, and Gaddafi in Libya ignored the religious-oriented powerful bodies in their enthusiasm to introduce Ba'athist socialism quickly in a society where Islamic rigidity prevailed. This annoyed the old religious leaders who promoted radical youngsters who brought out imaginary social exploitation issues and fanned fundamentalism which affected all the countries.

In science and technology, the young have a tremendous advantage as they think differently to bring improvements. All the recent technological revolutions in Silicon Valley are led by young people. The same is true in the case of engineering and medicine. Young minds are flexible, and in a situation where innovation is not a result of huge capital expenditure but due to thinking and software inputs, the youth have an advantage. This is totally different in social issues where the elderly have to be recognized, respected and given due place to get the best out of them.

In eastern societies, this is very significant and they serve the additional role of maintaining checks and balances in society. In western societies, for solving disputes, people have to take a legal route through courts, lawyers, judiciary and so on. The approach is clinical in contrast to many of the non-criminal disputes in India, China and other Asian and African countries where it is solved by village elders, panchayats, community leaders and religious heads. It has social acceptance and in many places, legal sanction. The power of the old is best utilized when they are kept engaged. Idleness leads to areas of concern. Concern leads them to exert their influence, which leads to social unrest in societies, where there are low levels of education; religious influence is strong and rigid attitudes prevail due to lack of discussion and debate.

India is an example of transition. During the freedom movement, the leadership was dominated by the old. Gandhi, Nehru, Azad and Patel had no great liking for younger persons like Bose. They felt that young people were more aggressive and irrational. The freedom movement's main theme was non-violence, and every act of Mahatma Gandhi was based on this concept of demanding independence by methods like non-cooperation with the government, fasts for long period of time and peaceful protest movements. The British was basically decent and rarely used violence to suppress this movements. They had great regard for Gandhi and other leaders. Most of the leaders had their education in British universities and were engaged in the legal profession. In China, the leadership during their liberation struggle was in the hands of people who had rural backgrounds. Leaders like Mao and Deng were from farmer's families and their outlook was less liberal but the common factor was that the elders dominated.

Gandhi was more comfortable with aged leaders and made sure people like Bose never dominated the Congress party. He had a fear that the younger generation may not like his non-violent approach and he was right. This goes to prove that whatever may be the approach; power of the old was a main feature in the two historic movements of the twentieth century – Liberation of China and Independence movement in India. This trend was also strong in the field of commerce and industry. To be in the seat of power, one must be a wise old man. Most of the members of the Board of directors were old men. This trend was more significant in the traditional Marwari-owned business. The main requirement was obedience and total loyalty.

In post-independent India, this irrational approach was successful as the old in the political field and in business were on the same wavelength. On one side, they were articulating the merits of socialism, controlled economy and the public sector. The same enthusiasm was shown to give licenses and permits to their favored few, and thus killing the entrepreneurship of the Indian people. This situation continued till liberalization of the economy took place which again was the work of two eminent Indians: Narashima Rao and Manmohan Singh. These two gentlemen were old in age and proved once again their influence to guide things.

In industry, the house of Tata is known for their expertise in running business on ethical values, yet making progress. In liberalized India, they made an impact with their progressive initiatives. The Chairman of the Company took the bold initiative of announcing the name of a young person, Ratan Tata, as his successor and inducting him in all decision-making bodies. This, in a situation where all the members of the different board of directors of their companies were all elderly persons, was an unprecedented action.

Ratan Tata wanted to make cars in their truck plant as he was a visionary, and strongly felt that there was engineering competence in the organization and cars would have a bright market in India. He made a careful study and gave a proposal for consideration and approval for making feasibility studies. The proposal to make the first Indian car Indica was given a lukewarm reception by the powerful old members of the organization, and it was to his credit and determined efforts that the first Indian-designed and fully Indian-made car by an Indian-owned company emerged. This initiative had ultimately resulted in making TATA MOTORS one of the leading car-making companies in the world.

After working in a Marwari-owned business, I realized the power of the old in an unusual way. The business was on the final stage of partition among the three brothers; our owner, being the eldest brother, made a proposal. He asked his younger brothers to choose whatever they wanted on condition that three young executives (one person educated in Cambridge, second person from Columbia and third person from London School of Economics) must be with him. His brothers chose highly profitable businesses and left the rest to him. He had no problems and was sure of success as he would be surrounded with people having ideas and not power-seeking dogmatic old veterans of the group. In many traditional companies, executive time is spent in briefing the old to satisfy their ego on small matters, and delegation of power is not appreciated.

In one of the leading, highly successful polymer products making company, the role of the two directors who held majority of the shares was interesting. They attended all meetings related to capital expenditure – technology upgradability, operations, marketing plans and such other things without fail. Their participation was limited to listening. The management was in the hands of business management graduates of IIM Ahmedabad and the delegation was complete. Here is an example of the power of the old to take initiative in understanding the advantage of youth.

One of the most interesting examples to understand the power of the old in post-independent India is the recruitment of one of my associates in a company located in central India where traditions were strong. He was called by the president of the company soon after his appointment to explain the functions of various departments in his previous organization. He started explaining and when the topic of industrial engineering came, he had difficulty in explaining, as it was not there in the company.

The president, being an old accounts-oriented person, had some difficulty in understanding industrial engineering concepts. He solved the problem by asking permission from the president to tell a real life story to explain the basic industrial engineering concept.

The president immediately asked him to go ahead and listened with great attention to the story of a horse during World War II. It was about artillery formations in the front line. There were heavy casualties and a young officer who had graduated from the military academy was sent to investigate and make a report. He took a thorough survey and made careful observations. He found that most of the casualties were among the men manning artillery pieces and concluded that if optimum manpower was employed in the front lines, the losses could be minimized. The important observation of this young man was that artillery equipment was manned by four persons, and when the firing was on, only three men were active and the fourth person was standing in attention position.

He asked the concerned persons what the role of the fourth person was. He was told that it was standard operating procedure and he was too young to understand the hard realities of frontline formations. The young man was not satisfied as he was convinced that if more than the required persons were exposed to enemy fire, greater would be the casualties. He was searching for an answer when an old veteran answered his question by telling: the fourth man's job was to hold the horse. The artillery equipment was constantly moved by horses, and when the firing was on, they got frightened and the fourth man's duty was to prevent them from running away by holding them.

He then told the president that horses were replaced by mechanized equipment but the man remained. He further explained that this was very common in industry where the technology or methods changed but excess people remained. This affected productivity, and that industrial engineering required time and motion study to optimize efforts and men to get maximum productivity

Normally, the best of the talent available is put in this effort. The engineers make elaborate studies to find solutions and after long discussions with all concerned, which includes trade union representatives, suggested improvements are implemented. The president was a man in hurry; he wanted immediate action. A meeting was called and he decided to go around the factory along with the head of operations to identify people in the *holding the horse* category. In a short period of three hours, thirty men were identified in this category, and before the end of the day, they were relocated or sent to sister organizations in the town.

This was possible due to the great respect he commanded over all people due to his age and long service. The unquestioned obedience, in traditional societies, to the instructions of senior citizens is common and shows the power of the old in such situations.

Management studies syllabus devotes very little significance to the importance of trust in running a business effectively. In China, trust is the central point for many traditional old businesses. We were in the process of negotiating a joint venture agreement between an Indian company and ANKURA, a Chinese company, located in Jiangsu Province, close to Shanghai. The first visit to their plant and the return visit of their executives were exploratory and limited to knowing each other. During the second visit, we started formal discussions for technical and equity collaboration.

We thought the starting strategy should be to make a PowerPoint presentation of our operations and the market in India for the products we intend to make after agreement was signed. We opened our laptops and were looking for power sockets; we could not locate them. The Managing Director of the company looked at us and told us that their management did not believe in presentations as it served no purpose. He added that, thanks to the internet, they knew about our company and we knew about their company, and requested us to use the available time to develop trust. The Managing Director of the company was a young person and he had inherited the importance of trust for running the business from his father, a wise old traditional Chinese Businessman. This company spends a lot of money in trust development with employees, with customers, with suppliers and all business partners. We spent the rest of the day talking with them during lunch, and continued our discussions while having dinner. This company firmly believes that everything follows once trust is created.

In India, many business houses do not give importance to trust and believe information-sharing and delegation must be restricted to the inner circle of family members and close business associates. Many make it a policy not to trust every person and subject them to unwanted checks on the basis of information they collect from various sources. This is also a business model which works however discontented the employees may be.

A Jain businessman told me a story of inculcating the belief of not trusting. A father asked his young son to climb on the wall and stand on it. He asked him to jump after telling him that he would catch him when he lands on the ground. The young kid jumped and his father moved away and the kid landed on the ground with light injuries. He asked his son to repeat the act, assuring his young son that this time he would catch him before he landed on the ground. The obedient son jumped, and once again, the father moved away and his son received more injuries. The father smiled at him and told him that he had taught two valuable lessons in life:

Lesson 1: Do not trust anyone.

Lesson 2: Do not trust even your father.

One of the leading business houses in India follows this policy. The executives of this company are highly paid, well looked after and well respected by the owners. The only thing that is not shared is trust. Even the top executives do not know the company's capital expenditure plans, product diversification plans, marketing strategies and other important matters till the day they are announced.

The role of all senior executives is to implement things without asking questions, and they are given full powers and facilities for doing the job. The decision making on important matters is the prerogative of owners and a select few outside the family. The trust strategy in most of the cases is driven by old members. It is yet another indication of the power enjoyed by senior citizens in all walks of life. Trust is associated with wisdom. Younger people, in their enthusiasm, trust people easily and face possible wrong consequences. The finest example of trust is the emergence of new class of young entrepreneurs in the Silicon Valley and the online retail trade in India.

Here, venture capitalists propel ideas into products by providing funds for capital and scaling up of operations. They take the risks for failure and their faith and trust in the capabilities of the youngsters is the driving force behind the success of these ventures.

The old enjoy political power in democracies by virtue of their voting power. In all democratic societies, the percentage of people who vote during elections ranges from fifty to eighty percent of the electorate. Most of the people who do not exercise their vote are the young ones, and in some cases, women. The older citizens are more conscious of their rights and vote in large numbers. The political class cultivates them to gain power. The recent statistics on the money earned by pensioners show that it is more than the average earnings of the youth of the population in countries such as Spain and France. This is an aftereffect of political clout enjoyed by the old.

Chapter 5

Making Presence Felt

People of all ages want to make their presence felt in the communities they live. In the case of retired people, this urge is more prominent. They led a professional life where their activities were recognized at different degrees and their presence was felt by the surrounding environment. Post retirement, they felt exposed to a vacuum as the transition was not orderly. The outcome was creation of many problems and the search for opportunities to fill the vacuum. Most of the people indulge in activities which were not in accordance with their true nature and landed them in a situation where the society did not recognize them, and this led to frustration and brought in an attitude of discontent. They used the power of respect to command their loyal networks to create a conflict in the society.

Russi Mody, one of India's dynamic business leaders, taught principles of management in a semester to us at XLRI Jamshedpur, a prominent management institute in India. He devoted three classes on this subject and told us live examples from his distinguished career in running Tata Steel. These examples were not in specific reference to senior citizens, but nevertheless show the importance of making one's presence felt to get right results in the field of management. Russi Mody, at the age of sixty, was one day made in charge of mines and collieries in addition to his marketing and sales function. He had studied liberal arts at Cambridge and the new function was of a technical nature with many problems.

The Tata Iron and steel company's collieries were in Dhanbad, which was famous for law and order problems. The collieries and mines were also badly managed and all the executives and workmen had a laidback attitude to work and the productivity levels were very low. The top management in their wisdom thought he was the right man for the job. He visited the sites and all the time was thinking about a plan to make his presence felt to kick-start the revival process. In his second visit, he felt that he knew the answer, and just before leaving Dhanbad, he asked the mines hospital superintendent to paint the hospital with white paint. The superintendent was a highly qualified doctor; he was told that there was no budget constraint, and he must get the job done before Mody's next visit after fifteen days. The hospital superintendent was wondering why painting was necessary, as the place was painted merely a month ago. In his visit after fifteen days, he went to the hospital and asked the doctor whether the job was done. He promptly replied that it was done and asked him to have a look. The hospital was painted with ash color, and Mody asked why it was not painted white. He replied, in a matter-of-fact manner, that in the mines area, there was always dust floating around and white color paint was not advisable.

Mody knew that this would be the answer. He asked him to submit his resignation immediately and made sure that he was relieved. He also gently explained to all the officers and men that a hospital was always associated with the color white, which represented cleanliness and, if necessary, painting had to be done frequently.

He was telling us that at that very moment his presence was felt and the message had spread at lightning speed – he meant business and no tolerance would be there on failure to carry out instructions. He followed it on the next visit by holding senior management meetings at a pithead to convey the message that the days of a laidback approach were over and started meetings in the conference hall only after the productivity levels reached the target. *Making one's presence felt is a powerful tool in any walk of life.*

In the case of retired people, if they get a feeling that their presence is not felt, they may indulge in activities which are harmful to society. There are numerous situations where senior citizens wreaked havoc and spread the message of social unrest on imaginary causes. A good example is the situation that has been developing in Ukraine over the past several years. In our first visit to this beautiful country, it was a part of the Soviet Union. Our team travelled to Kiev from Moscow in a train, and there were no visa requirements. The business was in connection with selling telephone cables to the Ministry of Telecommunications and signing an MOU with the ministry representatives. The culture, language and way of life is similar to Russia, and in the eastern part, it is identical to that of the Russian Federation. The minister and the secretary of telecommunications were from Ukraine's western part and the officers were from the Soviet Union and the eastern part of the country. We observed that the country had a significant World War II veteran population and the economic situation was not good and inflation was high. The Minister of Telecommunication, a decorated soldier who saw action during the Second World War, was a powerful figure. His secretary had worked in civilian establishments connected with the war effort. Our official meeting started on the date of arrival.

We had a translator with us and, after formal introductions, the minister told us that he would tell us glorious incidents of the Second World War and continued his talk till lunch. Very little was discussed about the telecom business. During lunch, we continued to listen about the defense of Kiev episodes and it continued even after lunch. It was a great test for our patience, and fortunately, we decided on terms and conditions and basic structure of the MOU. The minister also told us about the problems of veterans and the growing discontent as nobody was listening to them. We signed the agreement and organized a boat ride in the river Dnieper for the next day. The second day of our visit to Kiev, we saw ugly scenes everywhere. There were demonstrations at many places by old people, mostly veterans, demanding separation from the Soviet Union, and utter confusion prevailed all over the city. We asked our representative-cum-interpreter to brief us about the situation and heard that the entire movement was led by veterans who even braved the cold winter to organize determined demonstrations for separation. During the communist regime, the veterans of war, although disgruntled with their problems – mainly not able to make their presence felt – kept quiet as any dissent was seriously punished. With the liberalization and support of Western European Governments, they organized themselves into groups and whipped feelings that were imaginary and liked all the attention that they were getting. We learnt that the leading political figures of the Soviet Union, such as Brezhnev and Khrushchev, were from Ukraine, and the public at large, were wondering what the agitation was all about. The hold of the old is so strong that, over a period of time, the false hope that all their problems – mainly caused by inflation and bad financial management – would be over if they were separated from the Soviet Union; it was believed by some people living in the western part and it became a separate country. The problems for Ukraine began and continue to this day.

One of India's problems is to bring the people following Islam into the mainstream. Muslims in India are patriotic as any other religious groups. The past history of partition sometimes brings bad memories and it will continue for some more time among people practicing different faiths.

Mr Sheikh, a retired person from Tata Steel lives in the Golmuri area of Jamshedpur. He is a very religious person and actively participates in the activities of Golmuri Masjid. People of all faiths respect him for his decency and helpful nature. He went to Mecca to perform Hajj as a true Muslim and is perfect in performing all religious duties. His favorite place to spend the evening after prayers was in a homeopathic dispensary owned by one of our friends, where we discussed things related to our work. Mr Sheikh was telling us that pursuing religious activities after retirement was giving him great satisfaction. During his second visit to Mecca and other religious places close by, he interacted with people from Iraq and Jordan, who were radical elements spreading extremist views. He listened to their talk of how Islamic religion had dominated the millennium – 1000 AD to 2000 AD – and only in the last hundred years, there was a dominance of western civilization. These are historical facts and Mr Sheikh had no problem in understanding them. However, they also convinced him that the past glory will come back and the caliphate will be established in Baghdad to control the world. He innocently believed that it may be possible. On his return to Jamshedpur, there was a public function to honor him, attended by about fifty persons of different faiths. While addressing the audience, in his enthusiasm, he described what he had heard during his tour. He was enjoying the attention he was getting and the pleasure of making his presence felt. In the evening, we gently told him his talk may lead to an awkward situation as someone can interpret in a different manner leading to social unrest. He understood how his innocent remark could ignite passion in a sensitive area like Jamshedpur.

In Jamshedpur, the steel city of eastern India, people practicing different faiths live peacefully. They have tight work schedules and work in tough industrial environments for eight hours a day. There are good entertainment centers, parks and shopping malls. People are busy and peaceful.

Jamshedpur has a considerable number of retired people who, after retirement from the different companies, stay with their children who would get employment at the same place because of their parents' service to the companies. Some of the retired people built houses with the liberal assistance from their employers. The biggest occupation of all the retirees is to reminiscence their past experiences in their working life with fellow retirees when they go for morning walks, shopping or accompanying their grandchildren to school or bus stand.

The second most important pastime is becoming a critic of what is happening at present – the deterioration in values of every conceivable thing, deviation from the standard of working they had set up in their working life in different factories. They don't have a great admiration for computers, automation, and any innovative changes that are taking place in manufacturing which makes the individual's role on the shop floor less significant. They are looking back at things with anger and looking forward towards the future in fear. Retirees was spreading the circle of concern on things they cannot influence. These people sometimes felt that they were leading a humiliating existence as nobody was listening to their views. In the absence of a proper outlet for their feelings, they are a dangerous lot and are capable of doing harm to the society just to make their presence felt.

My father retired from Indian Railways and took up an assignment with Tata Steel and worked up to the age of seventy. He was in good health and stayed in my house at Jamshedpur after retirement and spent his morning hours in the front verandah facing the road on which people working in various factories commuted in cars, motorcycles and bicycles. Many of the people who had worked under him, and whom he had mentored, took this road and he was a very happy person if those people saw him and said hello or walked down to him and said a few words about how things were going. With the progress of time, these visits or recognizing his presence became less frequent and he became worried. His worry was that they were not taking his advice to tackle problems and an imaginary feeling that things were deteriorating. My mother, in her gentle way, had to intervene and remind him that he had placed an able person in his place before retirement, and he should not bother about things over which he had no authority and get ready to look forward to a life of spending time with his children and grandchildren. She followed this advice by moving out of Jamshedpur.

Making your presence felt is an important need for humans and Maslow in his theory on hierarchy of needs covered it extensively. What happens when this need was not addressed by society? In the case of senior citizens, this need is felt more significantly as they are in a situation where loneliness is a constant companion and an idle mind is fact of life. In the latter chapter, how this problem was handled in China is covered. China faces social unrest issues in a big way due to ethnic and religious diversity and the ruling Communist Party is highly sensitive to it. Large populations of senior citizens, who are not very active, are given assignments which are honorary but very useful for social order – keeping streets clean, checking unruly behavior, upkeep of museums and similar things. They enjoy powers like imposing penalties and this gives them the satisfaction that their presence is recognized and felt. The aim is to keep them occupied so that they do not get fancy ideas to disturb social harmony.

One of the peculiarities in the outlook of senior citizens is the concern on a variety of issues. Not contented with the concern, they enlarge it by effectively selling that concern to fellow senior citizens. The ever increasing area of concern created by senior citizens is marked by another significant factor. The very people who are spreading concern have no answers to address that concern nor can they in anyway influence the outcome. Stephen Covey calls them *the circle of influence* and *the circle of concern*. These two circles have the same center and any positive step starts by reducing the area of concern and increasing the area of influence.

When we were introducing the use of cell phones in India in the late eighties, one of the concerns of our senior executives was that cellphones cannot replace time-tested landline phones. When we asked them why they had this concern, the answers ranged on many issues and the most common concern was that, in the absence of copper wire to carry the signal, the air waves carrying the signal would get reflected from the tall buildings in the cities like Delhi and Mumbai and there will be a mess. We tried to convince them no such thing was happening with TV signals; they were not convinced and argued on various parameters like wavelength, signal strength and many imaginary issues till such time that cellphones became a thumping success.

Senior citizens get concerned about earthquakes and volcanic eruptions in distant places; military coups in middle eastern regions and South America; and deteriorating standards of behavior of the younger generation and spread panic, sometimes very effectively. The unwanted concern is an approach to make their presence felt and a psychological need for most people to get recognition. During their working lives, senior citizens had avenues to make their presence felt. For example, showing efficiency in executing tasks, taking initiative, making suggestions and working hard were traits recognized by all institutions and rewarded.

One way of making the presence felt for senior citizens was to make people around them believe that they are sick and draw sympathy. This approach works for a short time effectively. They do research on latest medical supplements and medicines to improve the status of their health. In our study, we found that around sixty percent of senior citizens take nutritional supplements and exchange information on their effectiveness with their colleagues. Health for older people is always a fascinating subject to spend time.

People who had experienced good effects of supplements and alternative systems of medicine command good audience to listen to their experiences. These people are firm believers in the concept that health can be purchased and that sustained efforts like physical exercise and moderate eating habits are not required. They become champions for spreading this theme in their own groups about combination of vitamin supplements, calcium tablets and the latest inputs from internet on the effectiveness of latest medicines for the aged.

The latest trend is improving health through natural substances such as garlic, turmeric, ginger, spices, and lemon grass oil. The underlying factor for all these approaches is the soft option and avoiding the hard route of regular physical exercise, walking, yoga and so on.

One of the interesting developments in modern India is the explosive growth of think tanks, committees, expert groups and such other bodies, mostly manned by retired politicians, bureaucrats, retired Army officers, persons from judiciary and academic institutions. One such body was headed by my friend who enjoyed the rank of Minister of state; the objective of this setup was to find ways and means to reduce child labor. His office was close to my office at Delhi, and one day, I accepted his invitation to spend some time with him and have lunch.

When I walked in, I was disturbed to see some ten people sitting on their chairs with empty desks and absolutely doing nothing. His secretary took me inside his chamber. We exchanged pleasantries, and I raised question of nil activity in his establishment. He was surprised, and as a matter of fact, told me his establishment was meant for not doing anything, and it was established as a reward for his past services to the party and the trade union movement of the party. Pariksit – name changed for the purpose of privacy – told me about how he had joined the Congress party when Sanjay Gandhi was in power. He had closed his hosiery trading business and joined the group close to Sanjay Gandhi, as he liked his vision and getting things done quickly and was extremely loyal to him. Later on, he played an important role in the trade union movement and safety bodies of the government. He settled down at Faridabad and was not enjoying the idleness after hectic activity. People close to him realized his potential to disturb things and arranged this activity for him which suited him. There was money, prestige and he was invited by different embassy counsels for labor and social welfare and he was enjoying everything. He was also sure the tenure for this committee would be extended by two years.

Pariksit told me that in Delhi on any day there could be at least around a hundred such committees of various types working on subjects ranging from focus on the Pacific Ocean to the effect of climate change in Uttarakhand. Most of the members enjoy good lives and are happy for being rewarded and keeping quiet, and at the end, produce reports which in any case will never be given importance. A classic example is the dozens of reports produced on goods and services tax during the last several years and is still continuing. This is the easier and harmless part of the problem. The members do no harm, and the only negative element is that huge money is continuously spent on such activities, and a culture of not doing work and still being paid was spread in Delhi.

This type of activity can have disastrous consequences if the members want to make their presence felt and give advice which is irrelevant and then the government might act on it. One such possible act was creating an impression that the law and order problem in the central Indian belt, which includes areas in Chhattisgarh, Jharkhand, Andhra Pradesh, Maharashtra and Orissa, was a terrorist activity similar to that of Jammu and Kashmir and should be dealt in a ruthless manner. Having been seated in a far off place like Delhi and coming to these lofty conclusions is stupid and cruel. There is no doubt about unwanted killing in the encounters where Naxals are responsible, but it is equally true that these elements are not secessionists and traitors who want to be a part of another country.

The former Prime Minister made the same remark on the advice of the grand old men in many committees. Having belonged to an area close to this belt, I could observe the developments closely and objectively. These areas were till recently poorly administered and local tribes had no political clout. There was large scale exploitation by business men dealing with *beedi* leaves, Timber Mafia, members of the State Government administration and police. Tribal people's perception of anyone from the state was that they were an enemy of their interests. This was further augmented when state personnel exploited their womenfolk. Intellectuals, lawyers and student activists from Andhra Pradesh were upset with these developments and initiated activism and organized the tribes to fight for their rights. Leftist parties also joined them and brought militancy, use of weapons and organized violence in to their action plan. If you compare this to radical fundamentalist, religious terrorism one is not doing justice to the real facts on the ground. The leftist intervention has many positive dimensions. The sexual exploitation of women declined; property disputes are settled within the community; there is no violence at local level in the communities; they are paid proper rates for forest products and significant improvements are there in reducing alcoholism.

The old persons sitting in Delhi where rape and exploitation of women were a daily phenomenon have no business to offer solutions to a situation which they do not know. A disturbing dimension to this problem is sending security personnel drawn from areas where joining police and security services of the government is an avenue for taking bribes. This value system is accepted as a normal thing to do in their societies. When these persons take up the role of security in the tribal Naxals belt, they resort to their natural habits associated to places they belong. They become enemies of the local population which was thoroughly exploited by leftist elements. When we come to the bottom of all these problems, there is an indication that it is a result of senior citizens wanting to make their presence felt as members of different committees at Delhi, advising the state.

CHAPTER 6

Old Age as an Opportunity

THE GREATEST EMPHASIS ON THE WISDOM OF THE OLD IS an emotional perception and cannot be generalized. The more objective reality is that nobody will deny that senior citizens can make a significant contribution to the society in a positive way. Modern medicine and awareness of various factors leading to a healthy body are not only increasing longevity but also enabling many senior citizens capable of doing physical and mental work in a limited way. If opportunities are provided, it allows them to earn money and keep them away from indulging in activities as described in earlier chapters which harm the society. A reasonable level of activity after retirement, in line with one's state of health, increases the senior citizens' mental and physical fitness and gives them a feeling of self-respect, financial comfort and recognition in society.

If you are regular in your early morning walk, in the parks around Domlur in the city of Bangalore and observe things, a familiar sight is the presence of kids under ten years of age tracking your movements. The senior citizens with good fitness are likely to be approached by these youngsters and given a pamphlet. These youngsters are well-trained and their duty hours are from 5:00 am to 7:00 am, and politeness and a smile on their face are their trademarks. They are keen observers and capable of evaluating senior citizens' physical fitness level. They eliminate persons of questionable health and focus on persons with reasonable health after watching their physical movements for a few days. These youngsters are the front line recruiters of HR companies specializing in providing part-time employees to various companies operating in software, manufacturing and media.

In a city like Bangalore, there is an endless requirement for part-time employees with different skill levels. The employee cost is raising along with the attrition levels. The cost of training a new employee is also very high. The concerned HR companies did some out-of-the-box thinking and zeroed in on senior citizens. To start with, Bangalore has a high density of retired people with particular skills due to several reasons: some of the retirees have invested in a house after spending a great portion of their resources and settled down in the city; some are permanently staying with their children after retirement. These two categories of people are on a lookout for a job which they can do to the extent that their health would permit.

The HR company then evolved a strategy to create a win-win situation for employers and potential part-time employees very wisely. The pamphlet given to potential retired part-time employees by frontline recruiters is essentially an invitation letter to attend a breakfast meeting at a posh hotel situated in the locality, with a request to bring their resume and contact details. The next step in the process is on the day of the breakfast meeting – the real HR professionals take over the things. It starts with a pep talk about how they made it their mission to serve the senior citizens and soon begin the matching of their skills with the requirements of employers.

The outcome of this approach is amazing. For the HR Firm, the costs are minimal; they have eliminated headhunting expenditure to the barest minimum. There is no advertisement expense. For the employers, there is no induction or training cost; labor cost is minimized; attrition levels are lowest; no statutory provisions like provident fund, gratuity and health insurance costs to be incurred. The senior citizens are able to get social recognition and get some money. The greatest contribution to this exercise is keeping some senior citizens occupied, and thus contributing to wealth creation and preventing them from indulging in activities which may be harmful to social harmony.

In a controlled economy like China, there are restrictions on media, Internet and freedom of expression. In such a situation, there is ever-present possibility of major social unrest waiting to happen with a light trigger. The western media are speculating such a thing for the last thirty years. The so-called free nations did many things to fan discontent in China in the name of supporting civil liberties.

They gave asylum to people causing unrest and encouraged dissent in universities. There is not a day without criticism of the Chinese Economy, the stock market, the collapse of the political system and power struggle in the party higher ups. The so-called bubble burst and slowdown of the Chinese Economy has been predicted for the last thirty years. The fact is that but for Tiananmen Square agitation, Chinese society is like another developed country with good governance. China has marched to superpower status smoothly and quickly. The transition from export-led growth to domestic consumption-led growth is progressing well.

The Chinese administrators and politicians are clever people, and they knew too well that social unrest could derail economic and social advancement. They had a plan to tackle this situation. Deng Xiao Ping's answer to this was the One-Child policy under the pretext that population is the main problem and an obstruction to China's march to greatness. The idea was sold to the Chinese masses very easily as it was a fact and appreciated by the people. The One-Child policy was implemented in a ruthless fashion successfully without social unrest, unlike other countries like India where population control measures were a failure. The population control measures like the One-Child policy was a facade for a much bigger objective which was to keep senior citizens occupied and giving no scope for idle thinking. The One-Child policy was accompanied by a drive to create jobs for everyone by various measures like export-led growth, a cheap destination for manufacturing, and high emphasis on infrastructure built up.

What happens in a society where all young men and women are employed, and they have only one child? The parent's total affection is concentrated on the child, and they look forward to a safe custody of the child during their working hours. In China, the grandparents filled this void very effectively. The children of working parents in China are not put in crèches to be looked after by indifferent attendants, while parents are at work. They get an enormous amount of love and affection from their grandparents who take care of them in their growing years; sometimes it is more than parental love, and they grow up to be law-abiding and responsible citizens. The traditional values which are time-tested are passed on to the next generation.

The greatest contribution of the One-Child policy to China was not the control of the population. In normal conditions, population control would have eventually occurred over an extended period of time due to factors such as increased standard of living, higher literacy, urbanization and better quality of life.

The benefit of preventing social unrest by having a large number of retired people actively engaged to look after their grandchildren is the hallmark of China's One-Child policy which is deliberately understated. The rapid urbanization of China (Target – seventy percent of the population) helped this process. In 2050, China will have 600 million elderly people aged sixty and above. This will be one-third of the population. This is a staggering figure and a challenge for the rulers. The planners are gearing up for this situation. The past history of the potential capability of the old to trigger social unrest is ever-present in their mind.

The Chinese Communist Party is very sensitive to the issue of the social turmoil of even a minor nature for two reasons. It is a matter of prestige to show the world that Chinese society is orderly, keeping with the prestige of the second superpower. The second, equally important reason is that Western European democracies and the U.S., in particular, are waiting to blow up beyond proportions at the smallest unrest – Western media gave more prominence to a Tibetan dissident climbing a lamp post than the best organized Olympic games the world has ever witnessed, at Beijing.

To keep the senior citizens engaged when the One-Child policy aftereffects become less significant, the government is putting great emphasis on the development of a market for care and entertainment services for the elderly funded by the state, and to a small extent, by the private sector. Elderly people are encouraged to develop the business of accessible healthcare, entertainment and physical fitness. The Disney lands for the elderly are daycare centers that organize physical therapy, dance lessons, singing groups, and other activities such as English lessons, painting classes and chess for a small fee. This is an effort by the elderly for the elderly encouraged by the state. The expectations are that it would keep at least five million elderly citizens actively engaged. The Chinese culture is based on Confucian values like caring for others and harmony, and this helped the process.

The other major step taken by the policymakers is to use the services of the old in urban areas by allocating areas to the local authorities to maintain cleanliness, safety, ambulance services, greenery, playgrounds, parks and law and order at grass root level through senior citizen initiative. It is not purely voluntary effort. The senior citizens are compensated by free passes to use city buses, theater admission and other freebies. They enjoy limited powers like imposing penalties for dirtying public areas, drunken behavior and causing public nuisance.

In a small area of Pudong – a part of Shanghai consisting of 1,200 houses – a group of hundred old women and men leads these efforts, and the outcome is very much visible. The state is able to keep senior citizens occupied in doing a good cause at a fraction of the cost if these efforts were driven by a department of the municipality.

The retired people from the PLA, retirees from the government organizations and people from police and paramilitary organizations who have completed their tenure are very active in this field. They are well-trained and indoctrinated in the values of discipline. They use their abilities to implement effectively the tasks given to them.

In India, things are not organized so far for utilizing the services of the old. The older persons cannot cause social turmoil as democracy is a very useful outlet for their grievances. It is a debatable topic whether these liberties in a backward country are in any way helping to overcome poverty, maintaining cleanliness drive, improving discipline and avoiding useless discussions. Steady improvements should follow the natural course of evolution and not imposed. These are western liberal values that are practiced in countries which are prosperous and have the luxury of good education, high standard of living and urbanized societies.

A small beginning is taking place in the southern Indian state of Kerala. This state has an acute labor shortage and is becoming a favorite tourist destination. The tourism industry needs a large number of people, and the answer is to employ part-time retired people. On the way to Munnar, where a large number of tourists visit because of its natural beauty, you will find a number of eating joints catering to tourists. What surprises you is all of the employees are mostly senior citizens. They are smartly dressed, clean in their way of working and give reasonably good service; the obvious question is why it is not happening in other tourist destinations. The answer is factors like full literacy, a strong and effective policy on child labor supported by all citizens and the reluctance of younger citizens to take up jobs as waiters that is not there in other states.

The senior citizens working in these places are paid a decent wage, work for four hours a day and get free tea and refreshments. Kerala has addressed the problem of labor shortage due to a tourist boom and created a win-win situation. The senior citizens who work in these places are a happy lot; they earn money, command respect, and the most important thing is that they are not participating in the endless rallies organized by political parties on issues that are not local. The communist parties used to organize rallies on matters like American imperialism committing atrocities in Cuba, Angola and Ethiopia and such issues.

The old retirees were the audience waving red flags and shouting slogans. These people were not committed to any ideology and use it as a time spending device. They are literate and understand what the speaker is talking and take part in these rallies as they are idle, and attendance is entertainment. The slow death of communist parties who held dominant political position and ruled the state is a result of non-availability of senior citizens who are usefully occupied in the tourist industry. In the earlier days, it was impossible to start a small business in Kerala: One has to face daily demonstrations of workers waving red flags even before the company starts operation; it would be followed by demands for higher wages, lesser working hours and further demand for recruiting more workers.

The most active role of the union leaders was to encourage workers not to work. The fact that tourism is booming and able to face a labor shortage and effectively face problems is a tribute to the policy of employing retirees wherever possible. In India, unlike China, the dimension of the problem associated with social unrest is less severe, thanks to democracy. Nevertheless, senior citizens have to be kept occupied by ways suitable to Indian economy and social customs. The biggest problem is the fatalistic attitude towards life, and any problem of old age is accepted as a result of karma (past sins). This strong belief has some positive effect on moral conduct and harmful effect on one's determination to increase the standard of living in old age and making a contribution to the common good. This attitude gets a boost in the later years of life in developing a calm attitude. This is a socio-religious problem and has to be addressed appropriately, and the negative attitude must be marginalized.

The success story of China in removing poverty, and to a certain extent, the current attempt to eradicate poverty in India is mainly as a result of firing economic engines on all cylinders in full force. This is possible by using all human resources – young, old, men, and women. The optimum utilization of all these resources is by finding an opportunity to work by having required skills. The first step is to limit population growth. The second step is making everyone participate in the growth process. History is a witness to this fact.

In western societies, the progress in economic terms and social equality leapfrogged when most of the women of working age were actively engaged in work and ceased to be in only child producing roles. The progress in woman's education followed, and the emergence of a culture of liberal human values was a further step in progress. This development is happening in India and China. Forty-eight percentage of the population actively engaged in producing wealth is the biggest factor for human progress. The fact that certain countries in the Middle East did not make progress in human development is due to the fact that nearly fifty percent of their population was not participating in nation building and restricting their role to child production, due to radical religious beliefs. These countries may have huge natural resources and wealth but keeping a high percentage of population away from work and denying them a voice in decision making is bound to create stagnated societies.

A study indicates that by the year 2050, forty-five percent of citizens in China would be in the sixty-five years-plus category. If the population of China stabilizes at 1.4 billion people by that time, the number of older people (over sixty-five years of age) will be six hundred thirty million people, who are a great number. In the absence of finding any solution, many of them will be idle, although they may have a reasonably good health. In such a scenario, we may not be using this valuable resource. There is, no doubt, some out-of-the-box thinking is required. We had discussed a few approaches to address the problem, but they address only the fringe of the problem. A bold initiative is required. There could be many contemporary approaches and some could be for specific sections.

One of the outcomes of the fourth industrial revolution that has begun is enabling people to work from home, not only in software operations, but also in other areas such as design, manufacturing, customer relations management, analytics and other such areas. This is due to progress in fast computing, 3D printing and the acceptance of the concept of sharing resources when they are idle, pioneered by Uber. The only limitation in this model is a requirement for minimum skills. I visualize the possibility of keeping retired people engaged, in line with their energy levels and health condition. The challenge of giving them skills is not going to be difficult as all the technology developments are user-friendly. The usage of smartphones in India is a classic example. People with a low level of education are using smartphones very effectively in rural areas for getting the optimum price for their agricultural products. They are using them for weather information, soil health and other reasons, proving technology use was not the monopoly of the educated.

The advent of the fourth industrial revolution would bring a transformation in the way people are engaged in the working life to generate income and raise families. The days of a permanent job with current career prospects for climbing up the ladder will be confined to government jobs. Due to rapid technological obsolescence, one would be changing jobs at least five times in working life. All employers will allocate significant budgets for training and upgradability of skills. The education system, which focuses on specialization after the secondary level will give way to broad generalization at all levels.

In a highly-specialized field of medicine, a doctor has to learn about robotics, software programming, analytics and similar things. The ability of a physician in tomorrow's world is not only a factor of his knowledge about the human body but also his integration skills of related technologies that will enable him or her to use facilities effectively. Integration of technologies and human abilities will be the driving force in the future, and domain knowledge expertise role will be largely confined to that of facilitator in the integration process.

Talking about senior citizens, it is likely that working life of individuals in most of the jobs will be subdivided into two phases: The first phase will be possibly in the eighteen-to-fifty years age span. This phase will be very similar to what it is today – fixed working hours, minimum hourly or monthly wage, and contributions to pension, health insurance and other social security benefits by the employer. The employee must also follow rules and regulations which guide employment. In this phase, it will be mandatory for the employee to upgrade continuously skills in line with technological developments.

The average lifespan in the foreseeable future will rise to ninety years, and it is necessary in the interest of social harmony to make social security viable, working life must be up to eighty years. The first phase is already briefly explained, and it is up to fifty years of age. In the second phase, the working life will be of the different order up to the age of eighty. It will be marked by very little training inputs (people cannot absorb new skills as they age), flexible working hours which in number of hours could be half that of the first phase; no employer obligations such as contribution to insurance and social security benefits and would require working in different areas in line with their skills. It must be remembered that imparting new skills is becoming relatively easier with advancement in digitalization. People can access inputs in an easy way due to advancement in presentation techniques facilitated by digitalization.

In this model, if we apply the suggested structure to developed and developing countries, including India and China, it will result in seventy-five percent of the population working at different levels of working hours and only twenty-five percent of the population would remain completely idle as result of old age and sickness (population of developed and developing countries is getting stabilized). This, in fact, is totally different to an estimated forty-eight percent of the population categorized as senior citizens by the year 2025 in many countries that are mostly idle. From economics operation point of view in the first phase of the job, people are paid for brilliant and efficient work and risk-taking ability, innovative thinking and the dynamism of youth. The employer pays for the benefits he gets.

In the second phase, the employer gets the benefit of connecting people to jobs which are temporary/one time, in nature, that calls for limited skill and enjoys the flexibility in hiring at optimum cost. In return, employers must allow flexible working hours, higher absenteeism due to sickness and different type of management skills to manage employees of fifty to seventy-five years. The essential requirement will be the need to develop software which matches jobs with people of this age group. In areas where working from home is not the possible, government has to play a role in the establishment of industries to suit the availability of this age group people.

Japan has successfully adapted to choose industries matching the population's educational and skill levels. Japanese education gives the high school level students necessary skills to get absorbed in technology-intensive industries. They have another problem of declining population. Japanese, as a policy, do not want migration of people from other countries to Japan for solving labor shortage. They have moved low technology industries to China, Vietnam and Malaysia. The overwhelming use of working population is in high technology products and services.

There is another dimension to dividing professional life into two phases: There is a worldwide phenomenon of widening the gap in wealth distribution. One percent of the population own more than ninety percent of the wealth in almost all countries, whether they are democracies, dictatorships or semi-socialist economies. This situation was possible due to a strong belief that wealth creation is a result of risk-taking, innovation, knowledge and entrepreneurship. More and more people realize that wealth creation is also due to inheritance, political patronage, analytical expertise and the support of monopolistic financial institutions.

This would result in a situation where the role of an employee in the creation of wealth has to be given due consideration, as wages are going to rise. In the U.S., the minimum hourly wage may go up to twenty dollars and this trend will be followed in many countries. From an economic point of view, this is sustainable for high productivity at prime age (eighteen to fifty years) of employees and in subsequent years of employment, wages could be related to lower output from employees and less number of working hours.

The greatest relevance of this model is from a social perspective with a growing life expectancy. People must be kept occupied for large part of their life, and an idle old age – due to age-related disabilities – maintained at a minimum level. This is essential as a result of revolutionary changes in medical sciences that keep people healthy for a significant part of their life. When a person is relatively healthy, he/she has to be kept occupied – remember the saying an idle brain is a devil's workshop. The model keeps a balance between economic viability and requirement of society to prevent a social problem, disturbing harmony in society.

A good majority of the educated people in all countries are realizing the real effects of meditation and yoga. They are practicing it regularly for relaxation and stress relief. A professor of yoga told me that Pathanjali, the founder of yoga sciences, has one important concept from the physical wellness point of view. He compares life to a fruit. Fruits grow from an immature stage to a point where they are fully ripe and then fall suddenly with all their glory to the ground one day. He meant that life should be healthy and purposeful till the last day, and there should be no scope for being idle due to age-related sickness. He emphasized that yoga is a path to achieving this objective. Imagine a situation where most of the diseases – physical and mental – caused by various reasons, including unhealthy lifestyles, are curable completely by medicine, and people are active to the last day of their life. The situation will lead to the creation of a bigger problem than solving disease and old age – the challenge of engaging people to live with dignity, the honor of being independent and productive.

There is always a section of the population who face retirement and living a long life without any problems. These fortunate few have impersonal interests, and they pursue those with vigor and enthusiasm after retirement, and they do not need the second phase of employment as explained earlier. Their numbers are growing yet they constitute a slight percentage of total population, in developing and underdeveloped countries. The second phase of working life is for those who need them. The efforts, of the society and state, are to create opportunities for such people as it is a requirement for happiness.

It is possible when the average lifespan goes beyond ninety years, we have to think about a third phase in the working life of people marked by a few hours of working in a staggered way. Compensation by employers could be in the form of providing an opportunity for companionship – free tickets for a movie, theater and museum; free organized visits to places of tourist interest and such other methods.

The impact of aged persons becoming productive members of society will contribute immensely to wealth creation and employment generation. The likely prominent developments as a result of older citizens creating wealth and not fully dependent on state social welfare would be in the following areas:

a) The pharmacy sector will be the first one to get the benefits. People will buy more health supplements as they can afford them and want to be active because of opportunities. There will be an increased demand for products associated with physical fitness such as treadmills and other gym equipment. It has been observed during our research that people who work out regularly are associated with sports activities preferred by the old people such as tennis, billiards, golf, yoga and such activities and devote time to keeping themselves fit. This will create demand for the health industry products, as new consumers emerge. The biggest effect of being active in old age will change the paradigm that associates aging with idleness, walking with the help of a walking stick and a drag on society's resources.

b) The second beneficiary of this development is travel and entertainment industry. The senior citizens are free from their family responsibilities such as educating the children and ensure that they are married – in eastern societies this is more important). In this situation, if supplemented by extra earnings, the outlet will be travelling to places of religious significance, health resorts, visiting friends and relatives and going abroad. Human beings, in their old age, are happy when they are not dependent on others or the state for any resource, and prefer to help others if it is possible to make their presence felt in a positive way. The pleasure of giving, however small it may be, increase with age and is possible if one has the resources to do it. Many of the charities and universities are supported by the money donated by senior citizens during their lifetime or their contribution of their wealth or part of it after death. In the modern world, where senior citizens are relatively better off than in the past, this becomes a significant factor.

c) The third sector of the economy which will get a big boost is publishing. Senior citizens like to spend time in reading and learning. Financial capability beyond the sustenance level will be used for this pastime. The advent of digital books where the font size can be adjusted to enable easy reading without straining the eyes would be of great help. Senior citizens are likely to spend most of their time before TV screens for entertainment and information on contemporary topics to sustain their reading targets.

The big change from a social dimension is the institution of marriage. Statistics show that if we exclude few advanced countries, an overwhelming majority of the people in the world have one life partner. Marriage generally takes place in the age range of twenty to thirty years and is a result of the efforts of parents or falling in love. The early years of marriage are driven by passion, physical love, romance, dreams, fantasy and many such factors.

When children are born, the effort is on raising them, giving education, and in countries like India, getting them married. Then, the process of preparing for retired life starts, and factors such as building a house and financial planning of resources are given importance. In the present scenario, where life expectancy is, say, seventy years, the husband and wife are kept busy in the above mentioned activities. There is hardly sufficient time for living together, companionship or meeting of minds. We, being materialistic, accept differences for convenience, and by the time you realize true happiness is in making choices and choose alternatives suitable for your mental wavelength, it is too late, and you reach your exit time.

In the world of tomorrow, where people are going to live beyond ninety years of age and are financially more secure, there is a significant period of the time after your children are settled to the time of your death. In this period, happiness is through companionship and meeting of minds and healthy acceptance of different viewpoints. In most of the cases, this is not possible, and a second marriage after fifty years of age becomes essential.

Happiness in the family is a result of relationships creating synergy by virtue of togetherness in doing things. In the early stages, this factor remains hidden because of many factors. Once the children are away, and one has to live with his partner, and there is a lot of free time, meeting minds is the factor that decides the success or failure of the relationship. In the model that may develop as described, at fifty years of age, one retires and gets into the second phase of the job with lesser working hours and more spare time to pursue things of his or her interest.

They are also financially more stable and probably more prosperous as a result of the fourth industrial revolution. They have to live at this stage probably for the next forty years. The so-called advice of making compromises and adjustments between husband and wife to be happy is, in my opinion, a false argument. Synergy in the family by doing things together as a team has a viewpoint on different things, and obviously, these will be not the same in most cases.

The secret of happiness is respecting these viewpoints and doing things together. Compromises, adjustments and sacrifices are politically correct statements, but dilute the capacity of synergizing things. The essential requirement of synergy is having different points of view, respecting the differences and coming to an agreed plan of action. These things are possible when there is a meeting of minds. The problem in most of the cases is that it will not be there, and the solution is to change your life partner by finding a suitable person with the same wavelength and making life happy for the next forty years. In the changed circumstances, this will be normal and accepted by the society in the developed and developing countries.

The model proposed is an alternative to face the developments in future. The senior citizens have a tremendous influence in society in most parts of the world. Their longevity is increasing; there is an improvement in health, thanks to modern medicine. The percentage of retired persons by existing standards is increasing, and wealth creation in society has to be increased by extending their working life, and simultaneously reducing the retirement age to fifty years. This is a win-win proposal to keep the aged occupied for a good part of their lives and also address the happiness requirement in the later part of their lives.

www.ingramcontent.com/pod-product-compliance
Lightning Source LLC
Chambersburg PA
CBHW031256250726
48655CB00005B/2247